BECOMING AN
EXTRAORDINARY
MANAGER

BECOMING AN EXTRAORDINARY MANAGER

THE 5 ESSENTIALS FOR SUCCESS

LEN SANDLER

⁄AMACOM

American Management Association

New York • Atlanta • Brussels • Chicago • Mexico City • San Francisco
Shanghai • Tokyo • Toronto • Washington, D.C.

Special discounts on bulk quantities of AMACOM books are available to corporations, professional associations, and other organizations. For details, contact Special Sales Department, AMACOM, a division of American Management Association, 1601 Broadway, New York, NY 10019.
Tel: 212-903-8316. Fax: 212-903-8083.
E-mail: specialsls@amanet.org
Website: www.amacombooks.org/go/specialsales
To view all AMACOM titles go to: www.amacombooks.org

This publication is designed to provide accurate and authoritative information in regard to the subject matter covered. It is sold with the understanding that the publisher is not engaged in rendering legal, accounting, or other professional service. If legal advice or other expert assistance is required, the services of a competent professional person should be sought.

Library of Congress Cataloging-in-Publication Data

Sandler, Len, 1946–
    Becoming an extraordinary manager : the 5 essentials for success / Len Sandler.
        p.   cm.
    Includes bibliographical references and index.
    ISBN-13: 978–0-8144–8065–6 (pbk.)
    ISBN-10: 0–8144–8065–9 (pbk.)
    1. Personnel management.   2. Management.   I. Title.

HF5549.S144   2007
658.4'09—dc22   2007025385

Printing number

10   9   8   7   6   5   4   3   2   1

This book is dedicated

to the memory of my parents,

who were my first heroes

and remain my heroes to this day.

Contents

List of Figures

Foreword

I read *Becoming an Extraordinary Manager* after I had invited Len Sandler to conduct training sessions for my management team in Japan. At that time, I thought his style of engaging our untrained managers with thoughtful questions and using practical tools could only be captured in a face-to-face setting. This book confirms that Len delivers the same value in written form that my team received in a live training session with him. Everything about this book is very much like one of Len's management training sessions: straight to the point, in simple, real terms, and immediately usable every day. Very quickly Len settles the key question of whether management is a learnable profession.

But there's much more: Len does all the research but compacts it down to eight to ten specific takeaways based on the core principle of employee development. These takeaways are usable every day by all managers and form the basis of an entire HR program. Best of all, they work for our managers in our international offices. I personally restructured my employee recognition program immediately after reading this book and implementing its suggestions. This book is a super return on the few hours of investment in reading it.

Kush Mirchandani
Vice President, Brooks Automation
President, Brooks Automation Japan

Acknowledgments

This book would not have been possible without the support and encouragement given to me by my family. To my wife, Marilyn, and my four children—Lori, Melinda, Scott, and Craig—I express my appreciation.

Introduction

Extraordinary managers make the whole greater than the sum of its parts. They add value to their organization. They get extraordinary results from ordinary people. Average managers wind up with ordinary results no matter how good their people are. There are even managers who, unfortunately, drag their groups down so that they get ordinary results from extraordinary people. The whole, then, becomes less than the sum of its parts. These managers have little, if any, value. They don't really manage much of anything. They're "straw bosses." After the worthwhile stalks of wheat and other grains are harvested, straw is what's left over on the ground. It's used primarily for animal bedding. The term *straw boss* has come to mean a low-level manager who isn't good for much. Such managers have very little authority. They're leftovers. The term also connotes someone who is petty and makes things more difficult, not better, for employees. I know some companies that have more than their share of "straw bosses." I'm willing to wager that you do, too.

Overall, I've found there to be four basic kinds of people:

1. *Those who make things happen.* You can count on these people 100 percent of the time. No matter what the assignment, no matter what the obstacles to overcome, no matter what the deadline. They're always improving themselves. Their development curve looks like a skyrocket. I'm assuming you're this kind of person. Why else would you have bought this book?

2. *Those who watch things happen.* These people are the spectators. They sit up in the stands. They second-guess and play Monday-morning quarterback. You probably say the same things to them that I do: "If you can do better, you come down on the field of play where the action is." Of course, they never do. They don't want to get their hands dirty. They don't want to stick their necks out.

3. *Those who wonder what's happening.* These are the people who are always confused. Things are never clear enough for them. They're always waiting for something. They say things like, "I have the responsibility but not the authority." They want things to be given to them. On retirement day, they'll still be waiting for instructions and direction.

4. *Those that everything happens to.* These are the victims. The "Woe is me!" people. They claim they have such terrible luck. In truth, they make their own bad luck. You hate to even say "Hi!" to them. That's the only opening they need. They'll give you an hour's worth of their latest problems and their latest troubles. You wish you could hold a mirror up to these people. Maybe then they'd see themselves for the way they really are. Some of them have had fifteen or sixteen different jobs. They always say, "No one understood me. No one listened to me. They made promises they didn't keep. It wasn't fair." After that many jobs, you'd think they'd learn that their own behavior has a lot to do with their lack of success. But they just don't want to face the truth. So they play the "blame game."

Because you're a "Make things happen" kind of person, I'm willing to share my experience with you. I spent sixteen years working in corporations, large and small, and the last eighteen years as a consultant for many of what are considered the very best Fortune 500 companies. I've seen my share of good managers. I've seen a whole lot of bad ones. Too many bad ones. I've been an observer. A note-taker. In this book, I'll report to you on those observations. I'll try to talk in simple, commonsense terms about what's done wrong and how it can be done right. Work should be more than just work. It doesn't have to be boredom, drudgery, and something to be avoided. People don't have to go around talking about "Blue Monday" and "Hump Day Wednesday" and "Thank God it's Friday." There are too many employees who just put in their time. Kind of like prisoners in a maximum-security prison. They're just waiting to get released for the weekend, a holiday, or vacation. It doesn't have to be that way. The truth is, there's no such thing as unmotivated people, just bad management.

When the cake comes out wrong, it's seldom the fault of the ingredients. The odds are the flour, sugar, and eggs were just fine. It's probably the fault of the baker. Some bakers are good and others aren't so good. Some managers are good and others aren't so good. The best have special recipes that they've learned. They take ordinary ingredients and incredible things happen. You can be like that, too. I'm not saying that the ingredients don't matter. Get good ingredients. But it takes much more than that to be a great baker.

I'm going to give you practical steps to follow that can help you become a better manager or prepare for a management position. I know you've got good intentions. Everyone has good intentions. The problem is that *we* judge ourselves based on our intentions. *Others* judge us on our actions. So, rather than focus on building an understanding of good management principles, we'll focus on actions you can and should take.

I've heard all the excuses that managers give as to why they don't manage. Excuses like, "I'm too busy," and "My boss won't let me," and "I'm not going to hold people's hands." To understand how ridiculous these excuses are, let's put them in a different context. Let's say you were having your house painted. The painting crew was doing a terrible job. The radio was blaring, they were making a mess out of your yard, and not much work was getting done at all. You call the crew chief over and say, "I'm very disappointed in the work your crew has been doing." He claims it's not his fault because he's "too busy" and the "boss won't let me" and he's "not going to hold people's hands." My guess is you'd be outraged. You'd probably call the owner of the painting company and demand that this crew chief be replaced. You wouldn't let him get away with saying those things. Why should we let our managers get away with it?

Recently I asked several hundred people in various training sessions a simple, straightforward question: "Do managers know how to motivate people?" A whopping 75 percent said, "No!" If we asked a different question—for example, "Do salespeople know how to sell?"—and 75 percent said "No," wouldn't someone be upset? What if 75 percent of the accounting people weren't good with numbers? Wouldn't someone want action to be taken? I asked those same people if would they fire their manager on the spot if they were able to. A full 25 percent of employees said, "Yes!" What does that tell you about their respect for the people they work for?

So, why aren't there more good managers? We've got many good programmers. Most programmers are very capable. There are a few bad ones, of course, but the vast majority are just fine. We've got many good accountants. Most accountants are very capable. There are a few bad ones, of course, but the vast majority are just fine. You get the idea. With management, it's just the opposite. There are some good ones. But many aren't very good at all. They cause more harm than good. They discourage, demotivate, and drive good people out of organizations. They negatively affect business results and cost companies untold amounts of money to repair the damage they cause.

I can't tell you how many hours I've spent captive in an office while the boss brags on and on about how wonderful he is. He'd tell stories about his vacation, his family, his hobbies, while I sit there thinking about how much work I have to do. The boss is going "Talk, talk, talk," while the clock goes, "Tock, tock, tock." You say the same thing has happened to you? And it drives you crazy, too? Okay, so you know what I mean when I talk about managers who "discourage, demotivate, and drive people out of the organization." Why a company would pay people in management positions to tell personal stories and build up their egos like minityrants, at the expense of people's valuable time, is beyond me.

I talked to an employee recently who told me that her manager wanted to hold an individual development planning discussion with her. She was delighted. She said she had never had such a discussion and was thrilled that a manager would show that much interest in her. She did her research and prepared a lot of information for the meeting. Unfortunately, the meeting was postponed because the manager was too "busy." That meeting was postponed nine more times. She said she is now so disgusted that she deleted all the information she had prepared and said that, if and when the manager reschedules the meeting again, she purposely won't show up to try to get back at the manager. Employees should be treated with the same respect that customers are given. Imagine postponing a customer meeting because you're too "busy"?

Why Aren't There More Good Managers?

There are five main reasons why there aren't more good managers:

1. *Most occupations require some demonstrated competence, but management doesn't.* Many occupations require certification or a license, where you have to pass a test to demonstrate a certain level of knowledge and proficiency. To become a plumber or an electrician, for example, you've got to be licensed. Frankly, even a dog has to be licensed. What do you need to become a manager? Nothing. Nothing at all. You just have to be in the right place at the right time. Maybe you're the last one standing. Everyone else has quit and you've hung around the longest. It's the "Poof! You're a manager" process. Imagine if there were a "Poof! You're a heart surgeon" process. I don't think things would work out very well that way.

2. *Most managers are thrown into the fray without training or preparation.* They're given little guidance and direction. We invest little and we get little in return. That's the way it happened to me. It was very typical. I can still remember the day of the week and the time of day. We were finishing up our employee coffee break. It was just a normal daily coffee break. We spent the whole time complaining about management. They were fools, bureaucrats, out of touch, and cared only about themselves. The usual story. I got called into a vice president's office at 10:15 A.M. My first thought was, "I must be in trouble. What have I done wrong?" The vice president told me that starting Monday, I'd be a manager. I was floored. I said, "Why me?" I felt I was being punished. He talked to me about how much the organization needed me. It's not the kind of thing you can turn down. I remember asking him, "What am I supposed to do?" He gave me the classic response: "You'll figure it out." Well, some people *do* figure it out. A lot of people, unfortunately, never do.

3. *Everyone is, to some extent, a reflection of who they've modeled themselves after.* Parents, teachers, and older siblings have an obvious impact on children. Those managers we've worked for have had an impact on us. Some of us say, "I'll have to remember how it feels to be treated this way. I'll be sure not to do that when I become a manager." But most say, "This is what managers are supposed to do, I guess. I'm required to be

like the person I work for. That must be what the company wants." So, a generation of mediocre or poor managers gives rise to a new generation of mediocre or poor managers.

The challenge in such circumstances is to stop the cycle and break the "stagnant quo." Be different. Be better. Be wary, though. You may get in trouble. There will be plenty of people around with the dread disease known as "hardening of the attitudes." I don't think you can be any good if you're afraid to get in trouble or be called crazy for wanting to change things. As Nobel prize–winning physicist Richard Feynman said, "Here's to the crazy ones. . . . You can quote them, disagree with them, glorify or vilify them. About the only thing you can't do is ignore them, because they change things. . . . Because the people who are crazy enough to think they can change the world are the ones who do."

4. *Even after they become managers, people continue to be rewarded for being good individual contributors.* Knowing what people are rewarded for always helps you understand the way they behave. Ever read a manager's performance review? It's usually hard to find a single line about management performance. It's typically about the projects the managers worked on and the problems they've solved. It's about how hard they personally have worked. They're like super employees. If that's how we're going to continue to reward managers, as individual contributors, that's what they're going to continue to focus on.

5. *Truthfully, the job is hard.* Most people can become programmers or accountants with some education and some work. Management requires skill that a lot of people don't have or aren't willing to work at. The higher you go up the pyramid, the more difficult the jobs are. That's why the pyramid gets narrower and narrower at the top. Figure 1-1 looks at how many people can do jobs at the different levels. It helps explain why people who make it to the top are paid perhaps 200 times what people at the bottom make. If you're good enough to make it to the top, you *should* be paid 200 times what people at the bottom are paid. People at the top of every profession earn substantially more than people at the bottom. They can do things that very few people can do. That's the way it's always been. That's the way it always will be. In a free market economy, people make what they are worth. If that weren't true, the market would correct it.

Figure 1-1. How many people can do jobs at the different levels of management?

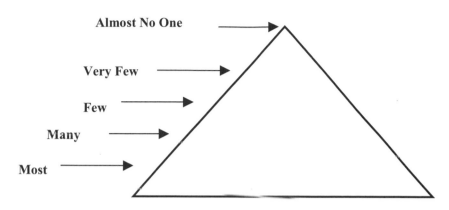

It Takes Work

So, becoming an outstanding manager takes hard work. There's no easy way to do it. There's no magic pill. There's a very old story about a king who said to his chief adviser, "Go out and find the secret of success. State it simply and succinctly so the people will do it." The adviser spent a year researching the topic and came back to the king with three books full of his findings. The king said, "That's not simple or succinct enough. The people are lazy. They won't read three books." So, the adviser spent another year and came back with one book. The king said, "That's not simple or succinct enough. The people are lazy. They won't read a book." So, the adviser spent another year and came back with one chapter. The king said, "That's not simple or succinct enough. The people are lazy. They won't read a chapter." Finally, the adviser spent another year and came back with five words. The king said, "Now you're talking. The people will relate to something that's that easy to digest." The adviser said, "Here's the piece of paper with the five words." The paper said, "There ain't no free lunch." The adviser was killed.

The unfortunate adviser was trying to relate the truth that success requires hard work, dedication, and good instruction. Imagine an athlete who thought he was so gifted that no practice or training was necessary. Imagine if the athlete said he was "too busy." The odds would certainly be against the athlete. You may think you can take the easy way out and win the lottery. The truth is, you have to pay up-front even to do that. You have to give up a dollar or two to get your one in 13 million chance to strike it rich. It's amazing how many people have a plan like "win the lottery" and yet they don't sacrifice anything up-front. They don't even buy a ticket.

As with any principle, there are exceptions. Some people are natural managers. But they're extremely rare. Like the natural athlete I once played golf with. I'm convinced he could have been a professional athlete in any sport he chose. He was that good. He had never played golf before. He barely knew which end of the club to hold. He hit a perfect 300-yard drive off the first tee. He turned to me and asked, "Was that okay?" I said, "That wasn't bad." The rest of his game was the same way. He shot par that day. The first time he had ever played! He needed no golf lessons, no preparation, no practice. He was a natural. Maybe one in a million. Some managers are like that. But the rest of us mere mortals need advice and counsel from those who have gone before us.

One of the problems with management training programs is that managers like to use them to "brush up" their skills and take "refreshers," thinking that somehow they'll get better just by sitting and listening. They see attending a management training program as an end unto itself. Most managers don't, however, practice what they learn. In truth, their bosses tend not to take training very seriously. Many managers who come back from training programs are greeted by their boss with words to this effect: "Welcome back from charm school. The work really piled up while you were on vacation. Ha-Ha!" So, managers may know the theory and not apply it. For example, I know, in theory, why I should hit a golf ball right down the middle of the fairway each time. I can't do it, though, on any consistent basis. My golf score isn't based on what I know. It's based on what I do. So, too, with managers. It's what they do that counts. That's why I'm not going to focus on the theory but on what to do. If you follow the suggested actions in this book, I guarantee that you'll improve as a manager.

One thing I'll often do in training seminars is ask some questions to try to get managers thinking. Coming in the door, I'll ask managers what brings them to the program. The most common answer is, "My boss told me I had to go." It's like a prisoner saying, "I know I have to put in my time. It's the price I have to pay for my crimes." So, I like to have them complete a few sentences, like the following, to get them thinking. How would you complete these thought-provoking sentences?

"I have a reputation as a . . ."

"Over the next few years, I also want to be known as a . . ."

"Important management skills I need to work on are . . ."

"If I improve in those areas, I'll be better able to . . ."

No matter what company they are from, people attending programs will frequently comment: "I wish my boss was attending this session," and "Does top management know anything about this program?" When people feel their management doesn't believe in or will not encourage them to use the ideas taught in the program, they tend to be reluctant to use them.

I remember early in my career trying to set up my very first supervisory training program. I read that you were supposed to do a needs analysis. So, I got a group of supervisors together and presented them with some standard topics. They said they weren't the ones who needed training. They said they were perfect in every way and their managers were the ones who needed the training. What did I know? I believed them. I got their managers together and presented them with some standard topics. They said they weren't the ones who needed training. They said they were perfect in every way and their directors were the ones who needed the training. What did I know? I believed them. I got their directors together . . . and so it goes. I learned the hard way that people love to point fingers at those they work for as being responsible for their lack of success. In truth, everyone at every level can be better.

Some people, unfortunately, may feel that expressing a willingness to attend a training program is an admission of weaknesses—that they might actually *need* the training. In truth, lifelong training is a necessity for everyone.

Organization of the Book

There are five sections to this book. They represent the major pillars of management. There are many other important things managers do, of course. That's why they offer four-year degrees in management. Since that would make for an extremely thick book, I'll focus on these "big five" after we talk about how to get the job you want and what to do your first few days of work. Please notice that these five sections are designated with Roman numerals, indicating their great importance, like Super Bowls.

I. **Motivating Others** (Principles of Motivation and What People Really Want)

II. **Attracting and Retaining Top Talent** (Interviewing: Choosing the Best from the Rest, and Retaining Top Talent)

III. **Planning and Organizing Your Group's Performance** (Building Capability and Accountability, and It's About Time)

IV. **Driving Results through Your Organization** (Managing Employee Performance, Introducing Change: From "Woe!" to "Wow!" and Maintaining Your Sanity: Handling Performance Problems)

V. **Lifelong Development** (Career Planning and a Look to the Future)

I encourage you to read through these chapters and look for the gem of wisdom that will help you. You don't have to implement *all* the ideas. But I'd be disappointed if you didn't implement *any* of them. Some might be new ideas. Some might be things you've known about but haven't done. Hopefully, all of them are common sense. Just do something, even if it's a small thing. Don't wait for someone else to tell you what to do. Don't wait for permission. As Mother Teresa said, "I can only do one deed at a time. So I begin. My whole work is only a drop in the ocean. But, if I didn't put the drop in, the ocean would have one drop less. Same thing for you. Just begin."

Moving Up to Manager: How to Get and Begin the Job

As you explore career opportunities, you'll probably want to draw upon a variety of job search methods. Obviously, you'll want to read newspaper ads, work though employment agencies, and register with on-line job listing services such as Monster.com. However, virtually anyone who has worked in the recruiting industry will tell you that most jobs (the usual number you hear is 80 percent) are filled through networking. That means reaching out to other people for advice, information, feedback, and referrals. It's a laborious, exhausting process that leads you into the labyrinth called the Hidden Job Market. Traditional job search methods are heavily tended by gatekeepers whose primary function is to keep you from talking to anyone in a position to hire you. Their job is to screen you out. You don't want to put your future in the hands of administrative assistants and clerks. The more diligently you work at your job search, the greater the likelihood you'll wind up with the job you want. Looking for a job is a full-time job in itself. Assuming you're still employed, it means working two jobs at once. Through networking, you find out about opportunities that are not published, budget requisitions in the pipeline for approval, operating needs that will soon be the source of staffing requests, and people who have the authority to hire you on the spot if they think you could help their organization. They don't worry about "approved requisitions" or "money in the budget."

How to Network

How can you work the network? Use both e-mail and the telephone (what's often called "dialing for dollars"), and then follow up, follow up, follow up. Assume that no one will actually do anything they commit to doing without at least three follow-up calls from you. Many people think that networking involves contacting friends and acquaintances for help, or making a list of anyone they've ever known and getting in touch with them. That's true. That's the easy part. Networking also involves cold-calling. Contacting complete strangers. Sometimes, using strangers to refer you to other strangers. The key here is that when you use someone's name, the other person will hardly ever ask you how you know the person whose name you drop. All you'll have to do is say simply, "I was referred to you by . . ." If you *should* be asked how you know the person whose name you dropped, simply say, "I asked them for advice and they suggested. . . ."

A good way to begin the process is to send people an e-mail indicating you'll be calling them within the next few days. It will be very unusual for someone to remember the e-mail, but it gives you a starting point. It also allows you to say to the administrative assistant or other gatekeeper, without completely stretching the truth, that the person you want to reach is "expecting your call." Once you get them on the phone, you want the conversation to go something like this:

- *Introduce yourself with a referral.* "Hello. My name is _____ and I'm following up on the e-mail I sent you. Do you recall it? Oh, you don't. I can certainly appreciate the fact that you get many e-mails each day. Well, I was talking with _____ (the person who gave you the name of this contact) and she suggested I contact you."

- *Explain why you're calling.* "I am a _____ (recent grad, career changer, industry expert, etc.). I'm looking for some help on _____ (be specific about what you need help on, such as your resume, getting a handle on the job market, learning about the industry, etc.) and _____ (name your referral) tells me that you'd be the perfect person to _____ (compliment the person you're talking to)."

- *Attempt to appeal to someone you are cold-calling.* Assuming you're talking to a member of top management, check out the company's website. Pick up some information from recent news releases. Go to the employment section. Find that person's biography and read his or her background and accomplishments. Now you're on your way. Talk to the person about:

- His or her reputation in the industry
- His or her sense of pride about their company
- Some accomplishment achieved
- His or her position in the community
- The views you share on an important issue
- A common organization that you belong to (e.g., you graduated from the same alma mater)
- A shared ethnic background
- Other shared life experiences

- *Prove you're worth talking to.* Here's where you have to hook them. For instance, you might say, "I have _____ (give a strong accomplishment that relates to the specific area you want to ask them about). I'm looking for some advice and would really appreciate your help on how to _____ _____ (market myself, write my resume, answer interview questions, prepare a career plan) and wonder if you'd be kind enough to spend maybe fifteen minutes to meet with me."

- *If the person is busy and puts you off, suggest an alternative time.* "I realize how busy you are. Could you spare just a few minutes of your time? I could come in early or meet you late or do it on a weekend. How about _____?"

- *If the person says no to meeting, make the most of the phone call.* "Well, I can certainly appreciate the fact that you're too busy to meet. Would you mind if I asked you a couple of quick questions now?" (Ask questions that you have prepared in advance.)

- *If the person has no time for questions, offer a compromise.* "Well, I can understand how busy you must be. Would you be willing to critique my resume via e-mail? I could send it to you. . . ." (The longer you can keep people on the phone, the more likely they are to agree to meet with you. Give them plenty of opportunity to do that. If they do agree to a meeting, be sure to send them an e-mail confirming the appointment. Many executives rely on someone else to make appointments for them and are very bad about setting appointments on their own.)

- *If they still can't meet with you, ask for a referral.* "Thank you anyhow for taking the time to talk with me. I'm sorry I won't have an opportunity to meet you. I really would have liked that. I can certainly understand why you're not able to give me some help on my resume. Is there anyone else you can think of who may be able to give me some additional advice?"

- *If they can't think of anyone, prompt them with an idea.* "Perhaps an employee of yours or a colleague in another company, or someone from one of the professional associations you belong to. . . ."

- *Close the conversation.* "Thanks for your help. May I call you again sometime, if I'm still looking for advice?"

Now you're ready to make your next phone call, and you can start out that conversation by saying, "I was talking to _____ and he suggested I contact you." What if you're actually able to get in to see the person? What then? Well, have a list of questions. Go in with pen and paper in hand. Here are a few ideas about what to ask:

- How did you decide to enter this field?
- What has been your career path? Is that typical for someone in your position?
- What do you like most about your job? What do you like least?
- Do you have any regrets about what you've done in your career?
- What are the important skills that lead to success?
- What am I missing in my background that would help me in this field?
- What professional organizations do you suggest I join?
- What does the trend look like for employment in this field?
- What companies might be interested in someone with my experience? Do you have any contacts there?
- What do you think I should emphasize in my resume? What should I deemphasize?
- What job-search techniques do you recommend?
- What kind of experience do you think I should look for in my next job?
- What conventions or professional meetings should I attend to make more contacts?
- What should I be doing in this field to get more visibility and credibility?

- Is there someone within your organization who might be willing to talk to me?

Always send an e-mail thanking your contacts for their time and telling them how much you appreciate their help. Keep good records on each meeting, too. If one of your contacts says something such as, "Feel free to get back to me if I can be of additional help," then go back to them at a later time, if necessary, and remind them that the two of you spoke.

How to Interview

What happens when you get an actual job interview? Be prepared to point out your achievements, show enthusiasm for the organization and the job opportunity, and ask relevant questions that let them know how interested you are.

Interview Don'ts
- Don't complain about anything.
- Don't criticize anyone.
- Don't interrupt.
- Don't give long, confusing answers. A good rule of thumb is that no answer should be longer than a minute. If they want to know more, they'll ask.
- Don't be vague or evasive.
- Don't exaggerate or stretch the truth.
- Don't discuss any personal problems.

Important Interview Do's
- Be early or on time.
- Relax.
- Research the company.
- Be a good listener.
- Talk accomplishments and results.
- Look and act like a professional.
- Prepare questions and answers in advance.
- Always be positive. Even with failure experiences, talk about "lessons learned" and how useful the experience was to you in subsequent similar situations.

Here's how to handle the classic interview questions:

- *"Tell me about yourself."* Interviewers don't want to know your life history. They don't care how many brothers or sisters you have or what your hobbies are. This is your chance to give an "elevator pitch." That's a thirty-second summary of what makes you so special. It's as if you were talking to someone on an elevator between floors. Hit them hard and fast with what's special about you and your work experience.

- *"What interests you in this job?"* Here's where you have to make a connection between this opportunity and your career plans. Let them know why it's the next logical step for you. Or give a more general response about how the job will represent a real challenge for you and why you're ready for it.

- *"What interests you in this company?"* Give a prepared response based on the research you've done about the company. Tell them about the growth history and the company's outstanding reputation. Use specifics that you have memorized from the website.

- *"Why should we hire you?"* There are few times where bragging is the right thing to do. This is one of them. Describe your best qualities and give specific examples of the significant things you've been able to do. Say something like, "I know this company is interested in creative, hardworking people. I'd like to think I fit into that category because I've been able to. . . ."

- *"Why are you looking to leave your current company?"* Although you might be tempted to rip apart your manager and the fools who are driving the business into the ground, don't do it. Talk about how you feel it's time to move on, how opportunity is very limited where you work now and you're looking for a new challenge. One of the top reasons people don't get the job is that they come across as complainers. Don't fall into that trap.

- *"What do you like most about your current job?"* In answering this question, make sure that you keep in mind what the job is that you're applying for. Be truthful and talk about the kinds of things you enjoy doing, but always keep it relevant to the job you are applying for.

- *"What are your strengths and weaknesses?"* The first part is a softball question. Succinctly describe the things you do well and be prepared to give examples of accomplishments. You have to be careful on the second part, however. You have to say something. It would be a worst-case scenario if you said, "I have no weaknesses." So, offer up a weakness that isn't really a weakness. For example, you could say, "I sometimes get impatient with people who don't follow through on their commitments." A good interviewer will ask you for a recent example of how you handled that type of situation. Be ready to describe what you did and how there was a successful outcome. The "strengths and weaknesses" question is a cat-and-mouse game. Don't disclose anything that can be used to reject you. If you want to mention a technical weakness, that's fine as long as you talk about what you are doing to get up to speed in that area or it's something that isn't required in the job for which you're applying.

• *"Do you have experience in . . . ?"* If you do, describe clearly and succinctly what your experience has been. Never give a "no" answer to this question. Instead, say something like, "I have done a considerable amount of work in . . . ." Then stress how similar that is to what they're asking about and how easily your skills can be transferred. In short, talk about what you *have* done rather than what you *haven't* done.

• *"What are your salary expectations?"* This is another tricky question that can be used to eliminate you if you're not careful. If there was a stated salary range, you can repeat that back to the interviewer. If not, you can respond with what you're currently earning. A safe response is, "I'm looking to advance my career, and salary would be only one consideration." In general, the less you say on this subject early in the interview process, the better. Once they've decided they want you, *then* you can start to negotiate compensation.

Interviewing is a lot like selling a product, except, in this case, the product is *you*! Rehearse what you'll say, role-play with others, and video yourself for playback and critique. If you're like most people, you're probably not as well prepared as you should be to present yourself in the best possible light. You want to maximize your chances of getting the job you want.

What to Do After You've Accepted the Job Offer

So, you're offered the job you want and you accept it. Congratulations. Now, you're ready to stop celebrating and start performing. Many people are overwhelmed when they get their first management job. They feel their career was on the fast track but now they're trapped in trying to do something they don't know how to do. Some wind up being fired or quitting shortly after being "rewarded" with a promotion into management. There are a lot of reasons people fail, but the biggest reason, in my experience, is that they keep on doing the same things they did before they became a manager. They get a new job in name only. What exactly *should* they do? First of all, as you climb through the ranks of management, your time will be spent more and more on the topics covered in this book. You'll leave behind doing the work and be involved more and more in managing the work.

Moving from individual contributor to manager is a difficult transition to make. As Figure 2-1 illustrates, it usually involves suddenly going from a senior-level position where you are spending most of your time doing the work to a junior-level management position where you are spending most of your time managing the work. Unfortunately, some people never seem to be able to make the transition. Others were chosen for management because they were outstanding workers. They've been terrific problem-solvers. It's just that they don't know anything about dealing with people. It's like the hardware and software of a computer system. They have to function well together so the computer works flawlessly. So, too, with an organization. The technical work of the department is hard. No question about it. The management work is just as hard. Yet both have to be done.

Many new managers make the mistake of thinking that their people are interested in them. They're not. They're most interested in themselves. When a new manager starts, employees have a lot of questions. They want to know how the management change will affect them. They want to know if their job will change. They want to know if this new boss will make their

Figure 2-1. The doing vs. managing divide.

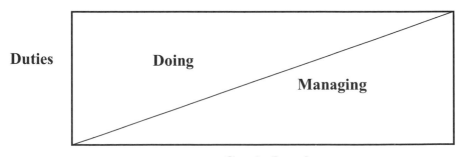

jobs easier or harder. So, don't come in talking all about yourself. Don't brag about your accomplishments on other jobs. Don't say, "Here's the way we did it back at the XYZ company." It will make people dislike you from the start. It's more important to be an interested person than an interesting person. You'll impress employees the most if you show genuine, sincere interest in them.

For many people, if you're a manager, that means you can't be trusted. They're like the cat that Mark Twain describes as jumping on a hot stove. A cat who does that is smart enough to avoid hot stoves for the rest of its life. Unfortunately, it's not smart enough to differentiate between a hot and a cold stove. So, the cat generally avoids all stoves, hot or cold. Some people will say about you, "You'd better not ask questions of the boss. You'll get in trouble." You might ask, "Why would you say that?" Their response might be, "Well, once back in 1983 I got in trouble with a manager, so I've never asked questions since." There are a lot of Twain's cats out there. You've got to earn people's respect and trust. It's not going to be automatically given. They care about your deeds and not your words. As a new manager, it's best to keep the rhetoric to a minimum and look for opportunities to prove yourself.

Recognize *your* new manager is on your side. He has a vested interest in your success. Therefore, you're in the best possible bargaining position when you're new to the job. You don't know what can't be done. People are on your side. It's a little like when the country elects a new president. More legislation is typically passed in a president's first year than in the next three years combined. So, go to your manager and ask for things. Say, "This is important to my people. I need this." It's unlikely you'll get everything you want. But it's very likely you'll get some of what you want. Remember, you have to *prove* yourself to your people. They want a champion. A warrior. Someone who's willing to battle the bureaucracy. We admire people who have the courage of their convictions. Try to fight the battles you can win. Back off if it's not worth the fight. But now's the time to push back. Your new manager wants to please you as much as you want to please her. The honeymoon won't last forever.

When you ask your management for things that are important to your people, avoid weak, tentative language such as, "I think . . ." or "I feel . . ." or "maybe" or "perhaps." That's like asking for a "No!" You increase your chances of getting what you want if you use strong words like "proven," "guarantee," "discover," "results," and "easy." If possible, use surveys, competitive information, and e-mails and other correspondence directly from customers. That way, you're not expressing your personal opinion but you're quoting facts.

Express passion for what you want. Your enthusiasm will be infectious. You can say, "I'd love to prove to you" or "I'd love the opportunity" or "I'd love to have the chance." Make it difficult for your management to say "No!" to you. Often you can tell them that what you're proposing has worked for you in the past or worked elsewhere inside or outside the organization. You can always ask for a "test" or a "trial" to see if it's going to work. Only the most change-averse people will object to that. Be sure to ask for things that are consistent with the company's values and your manager's preferences. I can remember having a first conversation with a new manager. This person stressed how we have to "get back to basics and do them well." What do you think I did in my second conversation with her? I came in with a "back to basics" proposal. It was as if she said to me, "You had me at hello." Just like a salesperson, use the customer's phraseology, jargon, and way of looking at the world. Ideas don't sell themselves. You've got to sell them.

Companies tend to hire people for a reason. More people are rejected than accepted. If you were chosen for the job, someone must have thought you'd fit in with the values, norms, and culture of the company. The burden is on you, then, to learn the jargon, the way of thinking, and the operating style of the company. Let's clarify these terms:

Values	General ideas about what's good and bad
Norms	Specific expectations about how people should behave
Culture	The pervading system of values and norms

The needs, prejudices, and reward systems in companies and the way they think can be quite different. What one organization prizes, another looks upon with disdain. It's as if you were going to spend some time in a foreign country. What would you do when you first arrive? You certainly would have learned as much as possible even before you got there. You would have researched the country on the Internet and talked to people who have visited or lived there. You'd probably hire a tour guide to show you around when you first arrived. You'd learn the local ways of doing things so you wouldn't stand out in a crowd as an "outsider." For example, imagine if you were a woman staying at the Intercontinental Hotel in the strict Islamic city of Dacca, the capital of Bangladesh. There is a sign inside the hotel that says, "Ladies in shorts may be stoned." No, that doesn't refer to drug use. It means that people would be within their legal rights to throw rocks at a woman wearing shorts until they killed her. If you drove a rental car too fast in Singapore, you could be subject to a $5,000 fine for speeding. A popular T-shirt that young people wear in Singapore says, "Singapore is a fine country." Now you understand the way they mean it. The last thing you'd ever do if you went into a foreign country is try to change their culture overnight.

The old-fashioned view of an organization was as a pyramid where the people at the top are the important ones. Information would flow one way—downward. The planning, organizing, controlling, and directing were all done at the top. The job of a subordinate was simply to support the wishes of management. Often, people would get a sore neck because they looked one way virtually all the time—upward. Employees existed to serve their manager. A more modern view of an organization is as an up-side-down pyramid, as shown in Figure 2-2. The people at the top (the employees) are the important ones. They make the product, sell the product, service the product, and work with customers on a day-to-day basis. Information should flow two ways—upward and downward. The job of the manager is to support the employees. Managers should get a sore neck

Figure 2-2. Information flow in the old vs. modern organization.

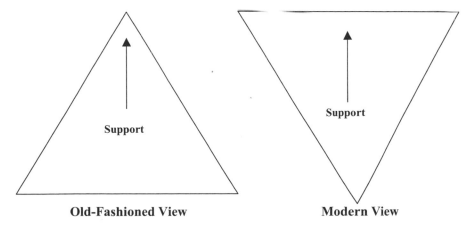

Old-Fashioned View **Modern View**

because they should look one way most of the time—downward. They exist to ensure the success of their employees.

You can show employees that they're critically important to you on your first day of work by having a group meeting. Don't make the mistake of thinking your role should be to tell the people all about your expectations of them. Just the opposite. It would be better to find out what their expectations are of you. Be humble and gracious. First impressions are important. You want to get off to a good start. Therefore, you should focus on them and not on yourself. The more you know about the department, the better off you'll be. Tell your employees how pleased you are to be part of this group. Tell them you've heard good things about them. If you're able to list some of their major accomplishments, they'll think you're wonderful. Remember, it's about them (the employees) and not about you (the manager). Why don't managers understand this simple concept?

I remember dealing with an egotistical vice president. He invited me to his first annual "State of the Nation" address. He got all 150 of his people in a big conference room and bragged to them about how, since he had come aboard, market share of his product line had increased by 53 percent. He showed all his major decisions over the year on a colorful presentation. He used the word "I" over and over again during a one-hour presentation. He gave virtually no credit to those 150 people. Because of that one meeting, he wound up losing his best people physically—because they left the company—and the rest mentally. Within the next year, market share plummeted to less than what it had been before he joined the company. He was a smart guy who didn't know much about motivating people.

On the other hand, I once knew a plant manager who certainly wasn't as smart or as talented as the egotistical vice president. But he cared about people. He knew every person in his facility by their first name. People felt it was a privilege to work for him. He was known for developing people and was proud of the fact that he had filled every management and professional opening from within. He always gave others credit and never tried to take it for himself. Through no fault of his, the plant had to close. I wondered how the people would react toward him. I was sitting in the back of the cafeteria when he strode to the podium to make the announcement. He stammered and choked up. He couldn't get the words out. All he could say is, "I'm sorry to announce that the plant. . . ." He started to run from the stage. As one, the 250 people working at the plant gave him a standing ovation. They were losing their jobs and they gave him a standing ovation. As I met with these employees afterward, they repeatedly asked me if he was all right. Imagine, their top concern wasn't about how they were going to feed their families. They wanted to know if *he* was all right.

It always starts with the manager. Imagine if I said, "I want my kids to love me, but I'm not going to love them. I'm too busy." It wouldn't work. If you love them, there's a good chance they'll love you back. No guarantee. But a good chance. If you *don't* love them first, there's *no* chance they'll love you. You get back what you give people. That plant manager gave and got back a lot.

The Job Stages

All managers will pass through a series of stages when they begin a new job. The pattern is always the same. Sometimes a stage takes a long time to get through. Other times, a manager can get stuck on a stage and never progress. But every manager passes through these four stages:

1. *Investigation.* The more research you do before actually accepting a job, the better off you'll be. This investigative work includes finding out exactly what the job is and isn't. It also includes determining what has been accomplished or not accomplished up to now and why. It should involve understanding the political climate and learning about the people you'll be working for and working with.

2. *Initiation.* This is the period of confusion when you're trying different approaches to getting things done. It's when you test people to find out what the underlying issues and political sensitivities are. It's also a time when people test you out to see what you're made of. They'll say things like, "The old manager let me. . . ." In truth, it never really happened. They want to see what they can get away with. Initiation can be an uncomfortable period when it appears there's no way you can learn what you need to know. Invariably, you'll step in some bear traps because you didn't know important background information.

3. *Acceptance.* Now you've adjusted. You've learned about your environment. You understand the informal organization and people regard you as a full-fledged participant. You're familiar with the department and company jargon and what you can realistically hope to accomplish.

4. *Contribution.* Only after you've gone through the first three stages can you really be of significant benefit to the organization. This is the stage when you begin to produce results and really earn your money. How quickly you get to this stage as a manager depends on how hard you've worked and how astute you've been in navigating through the first three stages.

The First Meetings with Employees

The biggest thing for you to do from your first moments on the job is to project confidence and optimism. If you're not confident, you must still *act* confident. If it's a problem department with a poor track record, then don't tell them you've heard good things about them and list their accomplishments. Instead, talk about how you're looking forward to the challenge that the job holds in store. Whatever the case, tell people how much you'll be relying on them. Establish the fact that you'll need their cooperation and commitment for success. It would be good if your boss attended at least the first part of the meeting to introduce you and talk about your background. If anyone is going to do any bragging about you, it should be your new boss. If people start to bring up problems, tell them that's exactly the kind of information you'll be looking for in your one-on-one meetings with them. Do not let this first meeting degenerate into a gripe session.

It'll be important for you to identify the opinion leaders of the group. They may have formal titles, but often they are just senior people that the others look up to. Be very deferential and respectful. Tell them how important they are to you and, if you can, run things past them before you present them to the group at large. These people will love it if you ask for their help and advice. When you say something, the more junior people will turn to these leaders and say, "What do you think?" You'd better have them on your side. You want them to say one thing and one thing only: "This new manager is good. I'm impressed."

You've got to take the time to build relationships up, down, and across the organization. Recognize that what matters is who you've been able to create alliances with. Grade levels, job descriptions, and organization charts are of little importance. If someone wants to ignore you, they will. If someone wants to put you at the top of their priority list, they'll do that, too.

During one of my seminars, a new manager once told me about his first assignment: He was going to Ireland to force those people to adhere to certain corporate manufacturing standards. His boss told him to go out there and establish his authority. I told him that he was going on a suicide mission. He didn't understand why. I said, "By all means, go to Ireland, but you've got to earn credibility. People have to see you as an ally and not as a threat." I told him to spend time at the pub with the employees. "They'll tell you about the problems they're having with corporate," I said. "They'll tell you about how no one got back to them on this and how they don't know the status of that. There will be some easy things you can do for them. First, earn their respect. Then you can ask them for help."

Think of the people who are good at relationships—salespeople. They know you must first establish the relationship and then you sell the product. I explained, "After a while, you'll be able to say to the people in Ireland, 'Can you do me a favor?' and they'll say, 'For you, anything.'" That's when you know that you've established the right kind of relationship.

"Why didn't my boss tell me these things?" asked the seminar participant. "Probably because your boss doesn't know them," I responded. "Maybe that's why everyone before me who was given this project failed," he responded. "You just might be right," I said.

I can still remember my first day of work in human resources. I was warned about a particular manager. They said he hated the HR department and it wouldn't be long before he tested me to verify that I was one of the enemy. Sure enough, about 10 A.M. my first morning on the job, this manager came down to my office and told me that he had submitted a salary increase for one of his people and never got the approval back. His employee was about to go on vacation and he was hoping to tell him about his raise before he left. I told him I'd see what I could do. I located his paperwork, and it turned out it needed his vice president's approval. The VP, unfortunately, was in Japan for another week. So, I called the VP on the phone and was lucky enough to reach him to get the approval. I brought the approved paperwork to the manager and he was floored. He couldn't believe I'd do a little something extra for him. From that day forward, he was my biggest supporter. I could call on him for any favor. It doesn't take a lot. Just a little interest in the other person.

As quickly as possible, schedule one-on-one meetings to begin to establish a relationship with each person working for you. Ask them if they'd like to continue these meetings on a monthly or quarterly basis. Ask the same general questions of everyone:

- How is the job going?
- What are the things you like and don't like about the job?
- What are your expectations of me?
- What's the best way for me to get to know what you do?
- Do you have any career plans or individual development plans that I should know about?
- Is there anything in particular that I can do for you?

Stress the same things you did in the group meeting. Express confidence and tell your employees how much you need their help and support. It would be great if you've done your homework and can personalize your comments; then you can say something like, "Jim, I understand you're the person who was responsible for the product innovation that led to . . . ." A lot of this homework should be done before you even start the job. If you can memorize people's names, job responsibilities, and accomplishments, it will help you get off to a really good start. Contrast this with the manager who comes in totally unprepared, gets people's names wrong, doesn't understand who does what, and knows nothing of the group's history. What a difference!

Be sure to take notes so that you'll remember who said what. It'll be very impressive days or weeks from now if you say to someone, "As you mentioned in our first one-on-one meeting . . . ." Don't feel you have to explain or defend anything that has happened in the past. If someone brings up past transgressions by the previous manager, simply listen attentively.

Be sure to use the person you are replacing as a resource, too. Even if previous managers left the company, seek them out after you've had the first group meeting and the first set of one-on-ones with employees. Anyone who previously held your position can help you interpret what people are saying and why. They'll also tell you about the mistakes they made with the group and what they found to be the best way to work with each of the people. You can also use new bosses this way. Ask them to interpret the things the people are telling you.

Make sure you and your new boss discuss goals and expectations. You may have to push back when your manager starts to pile projects on you. It's possible that you'll have to say, "I need to meet with the staff as well as internal customers. I need to understand the work and how it gets done.

Is there a way we could prioritize these projects?" Make sure you meet frequently with your new manager to learn her views on your department mission, goals, and expectations. Establish strong lines of communication with your manager from the beginning.

Hopefully, you've already done research to find out what your new boss's preferences and prejudices are. After all, the boss carefully checked your references. Shouldn't you have checked the boss's as well? You should talk to current and former subordinates of that manager. You should talk to reputable employment agencies and those in professional associations. You should find out his track record on developing people, encouraging innovation, and granting autonomy, for example. Don't let the manager give you textbook answers about philosophy. Ask for specifics on what the manager has done in the past. The company has made a big investment in you. You're making an even bigger investment in them.

Seek out the unsuccessful candidates for your job, especially if they'll be working for you, because they can affect your future performance. Put yourself in their shoes. Acknowledge their feelings. Then, take the offensive. If appropriate, tell them you'll make every effort to use their expertise and experience. Acknowledge that you need their commitment in order to succeed. If you're really good, you'll be aware of their achievements and can quote them. Ask them if there's anything in particular you can do for them. Obviously, if they are working directly for you, you are in a position to give them the experience and training they may need to enhance their candidacy for your position or a position like it. If you know they are highly regarded by others in management, by all means tell them that. The worst thing you can do is tell them how good *you* are. The best thing you can do is tell them how good *they* are. As a new person, you need all the friends you can get. You don't need enemies lurking around waiting to pounce on you.

If someone expresses resentment that you were hired or promoted or about having to "train" you, always indicate that you understand the way the person feels. Don't ever try to defend why you were chosen for the job. That wasn't your decision to make. Try and pivot the discussion from what has already happened to what can happen in the future. Indicate confidence in them, stressing how important they will be to you and how much you will need their help. If there is anything in particular you can do for the person (e.g., getting them involved in a certain project or with new technology), tell them you'll try to do that. Don't make promises you can't keep. That will hurt your relationship with them in the long run. Also, never argue with a resentful person. Never tell them they shouldn't feel the way they feel. They're already angry. You'll never win the argument. Instead, listen attentively and empathize with them. Try to be on their side, as much as possible.

Always use the "clean slate" approach with people. If they were known to have performance problems, tell them it doesn't matter to you what's happened in the past. You can turn around many supposed bad attitudes this way. If they had a bad relationship with the old manager, just tell them you don't know anything about that and you're starting fresh with them.

You've got one very important factor working in your favor as a new manager. You are your boss's choice. Your boss wants you to succeed. You also don't know the constraints on you because you just got there. Therefore, you're in an ideal position to ask for things. You're also likely to *get* them. So, be assertive. It will be difficult for your boss to say "No!" to you. Go in and say, "My people are very concerned about . . ." or "My people are pretty angry that . . ." or "My people say they really need. . . ." Look for the low-hanging fruit. The easy things that will prove to people that you've listened to them and you're responding. You won't be able to get *everything* you want. On the other hand, it's likely that you'll get *some* of what you want.

Opening the Lines of Communication

Establish a culture of open, two-way communication. The less information given to employees, the more active the company grapevine. Rumors, gossip, half-truths, innuendo, exaggeration, and facts get mixed together to fill a communication vacuum. While management is in meetings trying to figure out what to say to the troops, the troops usually know the story already and are trying to guess what kind of tale management will tell.

Be sure to look for small wins for your group. At the beginning, try to have your group take on easy projects that give them a sense of accomplishment. Save the big stuff for later. Do everything you can to make people feel like winners. Make sure their accomplishments are recognized. Early success will breed more success for you and your group.

Continue to hold regular group meetings. Recognize, however, that if there's a universal complaint, it's that there are too many meetings, they're too long, and they accomplish too little. In some companies, it seems that individual responsibility is avoided by calling meetings to talk about problems. The problems don't get solved. It's just that people can say, "Oh, yes. We had a meeting about that."

So, it's not just about running meetings. It's about running worthwhile, carefully planned meetings. It starts with coming up with the answers to these questions:

- *Objective.* What key results do you want the meeting to achieve? Don't just have a staff meeting to have a staff meeting. There should be a purpose to the meeting. If a meeting isn't necessary, then don't have it.
- *Timing.* How long should the meeting last? When is the best time to conduct it?
- *Participants.* Who should attend? Include people with decision-making authority, people whose commitment is wanted, and people who have a need to know.
- *Agenda.* What items should be dealt with? How will participants help in preparing the agenda? Who will distribute it? It really helps if the agenda is an ambitious one. Putting too many items into too little time will help people focus. The meeting leader can also say, "We've got a lot to cover. Let's try to stay on track."
- *Ground Rules.* What are the rules of conduct for the meeting? Think of the things that typically go wrong in your meetings and come up with agreed-upon ground rules. You may want to post those ground rules in the meeting room.
- *Physical Arrangements.* What facilities and equipment are required? How should the room be set up? Should we use NetMeeting, Live Meeting, or some other form of technology?
- *Role Assignments.* Who'll be the note-taker, timekeeper, discussion moderator, etc.?
- *Evaluation Method.* How will the meeting be evaluated in order to improve it for next time?

Figure 2-3 is a simple meeting evaluation form you can use periodically with your people.

Your management "bible" when it comes to communication should be as follows.

The Ten Commandments of Communication

1. Develop trust. It's not automatically given. It must be earned.

2. Openly communicate more than you have to or need to.

3. Be as specific as possible in the words and phrases that you use. Avoid empty jargon.

4. Supply whatever background information and reasons people need to understand assignments and requirements.

5. Be honest, but never speak against your management or the company.

Figure 2-3. Meeting evaluation form.

Meeting Evaluation

• Did this meeting meet its stated objectives?

1	2	3	4	5
Not at all				Completely

• Which portions of the meeting were most helpful to you?

_____
_____
_____

• Which portions of the meeting were least helpful to you?

_____
_____
_____

• What ideas do you have for improving this meeting?

_____
_____
_____

• Other comments?

_____
_____
_____

6. Actively share feelings as well as information.

7. Talk to an employee as one adult to another (the way you'd like your manager to talk to you).

8. Always solicit employee ideas, suggestions, and reactions.

9. Always follow through. No exceptions.

10. Recognize that the job of the manager is to *remove* roadblocks, irritants, and frustrations, not put them there.

Top Ten Communication Sins

1. *Commanding.* Ordering people around tends to produce resentment and anger. Statements beginning with phrases such as "You must" or "You have to" often produce angry responses (usually not verbalized to the boss), such as "Who do you think you are? I know my job a lot better than you do."

2. *Threatening.* Statements such as "You had better . . ." or "I'll be forced to . . ." encourage rebellion and attempts to beat the system.

3. *Giving Unsolicited Advice.* In most cases, the only advice that is welcomed is advice that is asked for. If you tell someone, "This is what you should do," most often the reaction you'll get is, "I'll show you. I'll do it my way."

4. *Using Vague Language.* If you say, "We need to come up with a better system," you'll only produce confusion. Is the employee getting an assignment? Is the manager going to do it? Is the manager looking for suggestions? Vague language leaves a lot of questions unanswered.

5. *Withholding Information.* Phrases such as "That's management confidential," or "You don't have a need to know," or "If I wanted to let you know, I would have told you" get bad reactions. Employees will think, "My manager doesn't care about me. I'll have to get my information from the people who do."

6. *Name-Calling.* Confronting employees by saying "You are careless" or "You're getting lazy" can produce defensive responses such as, "Who do you think you are to judge me? You're much worse than I am."

7. *Patronizing.* Compliments can be taken the wrong way. A lot of it has to do with the employee's experience with past managers. A comment

such as "I'm glad you finally got that project done" can be taken either positively or negatively. An innocent statement like "You're doing a great job" can be taken as insincere if corresponding actions don't match those words.

8. *Playing Psychologist.* Starting a sentence by saying, "Your problem is . . . ," almost always produces a backlash. Another statement to avoid is, "I know the real reason you're doing this." Unfortunately, performance reviews often set up managers as amateur psychologists trying to judge personality, intentions, and psychological makeup.

9. *Avoiding Issues.* This may be the biggest complaint against managers. We've all heard the refrains: "Let me check it out and I'll get back to you," and "Now's not a good time," and "That's not a priority right now." The employee response (usually behind the manager's back) tends to be, "Here we go again. Another issue avoided."

10. *Sarcastic Remarks.* Inappropriate humor that puts people down is usually met with hostility. An example is when the manager says to someone who's late, "I'm glad to see you finally showed up at work today." Managers often think, "They know I'm kidding. We have a great relationship. We joke all the time." They don't connect their sarcasm to high turnover, low productivity, and low morale.

So now you've succeeded in moving up to manager, and you do terrific work in your new management position. What's your reward? It's like pinball. You get to play the game again, but the stakes are higher. You do a good job with a group of five and you may get fifty. You do a good job with fifty people and you may get 500. You do a good job with 500 and you may get 5,000. The point values keep going up and the game keeps getting harder. Maybe if you play the game well enough, you get to be on the top ten list of players. That's the legacy you leave behind. You know what? That's not bad. It's something to be proud of!

Motivating Others

The Principles of Motivation

Motivation is a word that's used quite a lot. Often, it's used in negative terms. You hear about "lack of" motivation much more often than you hear about a person or a group being motivated. "My people aren't motivated," or "My hands are tied when it comes to motivating my people," or "There's nothing I can do to get them motivated" are common management laments. Do today's managers understand that *they* don't motivate people? The truth is, motivation is about what people already want. Everyone wants something. If you can give them what they want, their "motivation" will be satisfied.

Managers need to recognize that they can't make someone want something. Instead, they can determine what people want (i.e., what motivates them) and provide an environment where those wants can be met. I once set up an experiment with a group of students in a management class. I asked twenty experienced managers to define "motivation." Three of the responses showed a good understanding of this topic. The responses were:

"The drive that makes someone want to accomplish something."

"A self-inspired energy that results in a commitment to improve."

"The process of accomplishing what one sets out to do."

The rest of the responses, however, all referred to things the managers felt they had to do to "get people going." Their assumptions were that they are the active ones in the process and that employees respond to what they do. So, presumably, left on their own without a manager taking action, people would be "unmotivated." Some of the responses that showed limited understanding of this topic were:

"Enthusing and encouraging people."

"Keeping employees positive about their jobs and interested in the company's future."

"Praise, inspiration, encouragement."

"The ability to move people to produce more and feel better about it when it is done."

"Keeping them happy."

"Instilling a desire to learn."

"Giving people ambition to perform with a positive attitude."

"Working with employees to get them to work better for me."

"Getting your employees to do their best."

"Convincing others to have great ideas and then effectively execute them."

"Getting them to do the best job possible."

"Be their friend. Be firm but fair. Explain why things happen."

"The ability to get things done through others by instilling a sense of purpose and desire."

"Praising, coaching, and counseling."

Figure 3-1. Three-step model of motivation.

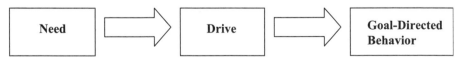

The majority of these managers showed they were missing quite a bit. We can construct a simple three-step model of motivation (see Figure 3-1 above) that illustrates just how self-centered and narrow their responses are. According to this model:

1. A *need* emerges in an individual that creates a sense of deprivation.
2. This need gives rise to tension and creates a *drive*.
3. The person engages in *goal-directed behavior,* which involves searching for ways to satisfy the need.

How or why that original need emerges no one really knows. And managers shouldn't really care. Do you know, for example, why a certain artist, musician, or dancer wants to work day and night to become the best? You don't and you never will. *That* person may not know. And it doesn't matter. All you care about is that the person has a strong need. The rest is predictable. So, you don't have to understand anything about the people who work for you or those you work with other than that they need something. If you can provide it, you're in business. You're a "motivator" of people.

We can deduce motives from the way people behave. Motives cannot be observed directly. Thus, we might observe someone attending night classes and infer a motive to achieve. Or someone might like to tell jokes at meetings and we infer a motive to gain attention. Remember, *why* another person has a certain motive should not be our concern. We have enough trouble trying to understand ourselves, let alone trying to understand how others developed their motives. If we're correct in inferring a motive, we then have a means of explaining behavior. Sometimes the inferences are right and other times they're wrong. If individual employees can tell us directly what they want, so much the better. We can then be in a much better position to try to provide it to them or provide a set of circumstances to help them achieve it.

Developing an achieving workforce that can adapt and has a chance of succeeding in today's fiercely competitive business climate depends on resolving the basic conflict that exists between what is needed to make work productive and what is needed to meet employee needs. Work is theoretically most productive when it is broken down into small jobs that can be repeated over and over again in the same way. This theory was the basis for scientific management and the manufacturing assembly lines introduced during the industrial revolution. Managers, quality control inspectors, and layers of bureaucracy would check people's work to ensure that mistakes were caught. Employees joined unions to protect them from oppressive management practices, and the cost of products kept rising. It was a system that worked for decades. It was assumed that people had to be closely supervised and employee rewards would come in the form of money and benefits.

Trying to have a motivated workforce today requires an entirely different set of conditions. First, the differences among people have to be analyzed. People differ with respect to the needs they strive to satisfy. The more managers can match the work with these needs, the more productive people are likely to be. A creative manager can find ways to provide for needs such as variety, recognition, sense of achievement, and autonomy in order to achieve both individual satisfaction and high performance.

Managers *must* be interested in motivation because it's their job to get people to produce a quality effort on organizational goals, whether these goals involve putting tires on automobiles, solving computer programming problems, or granting bank loans that have a high percentage chance of being repaid. Managers in today's organization pay a heavy price for not paying attention to motivation. The price includes conflict with employees, low quality, poor efficiency, absenteeism, and turnover. Motivated employees, on the other hand, contribute creativity, show enthusiasm, strive to not just meet but to exceed goals, inspire their peers to better performance, show commitment to customers, and allow an organization to compete effectively in the global marketplace.

There's a lot managers can do to motivate. But what's most important? What do employees want? Is it recognition? Opportunity to grow? Open two-way communication? You can't give people everything. What's *most* important to them? What do *they* feel they're not getting? Furthermore, are there differences between different kinds of employees?

Most experts agree that people want to satisfy some common needs—to make money, to feel important, to enhance self-image, to feel a sense of accomplishment, to work as part of a team, for example. How well these needs are met on the job determines to a large extent how much energy and commitment someone is willing to devote to the job. Ability isn't enough. The highly motivated person often outperforms someone with greater ability. Thomas Edison, regarded by many as the greatest inventor of all time, admitted he had limited ability. He said, "I fail my way to success. I just run more experiments than anyone else." He only slept a few hours a night and just outworked his competitors. In any field, the person with the greatest raw talent is consistently outperformed by those with lesser raw talent but greater commitment to hard work. Of course, the ideal is to have tremendous talent and tremendous commitment to hard work. We call that person a "superstar." They're not just worth 5 percent or 10 percent more than the average person. They may be worth 500 percent or 1,000 percent more. The only problem with these people is that there aren't enough of them to go around.

What Do People Want from Work?

Work is one of the few places where most of people's needs can be met. If management is somehow able to set up conditions so that those needs are met through dedication to critical organizational objectives, you can have something special happen. Look at the top-performing organizations or departments. You'll find that "special something" happening. Sometimes, it's fleeting. It might be a project team that spends a weekend developing something revolutionary. No one can believe the miracles that group performed over the weekend. Sometimes, it's an organization catching lightning in a bottle and showing explosive growth. Other times it's an organization showing steady growth over an extended period of time. Success breeds success. People want to be part of a winning team. When word gets out that your group, department, or company has something special going on, the very best people want to become part of it. Because you attract the best people, the success has a chance of continuing.

The key to all this is managers. They set the group goals, define individual responsibilities, and can provide many of the rewards and incentives that produce high performance. The challenge is that needs and motives can't be seen and can be difficult to measure. Employees can have difficulty articulating what's important to them. Managers then have to infer what drives people. Managers can be wrong in their inferences. Since they can't extensively analyze every person and situation, they should develop practices that motivate most of the people most of the time and establish open lines of communication so they can periodically ask people the following questions:

- What is it that you're getting that you want? (Try to maintain this incentive.)
- What is it you're getting that you don't want? (Try to decrease this disincentive.)
- What is it that you're not getting that you want? (Try to increase this incentive.)
- What is it that you're not getting that you don't want? (Try to maintain this situation.)

The matrix in Figure 3-2 makes this method easy to remember.

Good results are most easily obtained when people's needs are being met. If performance is low, managers should examine how employees' needs are not being met. Threatening people or punishing them typically produces only resentment. Rewards are not always provided for achieving appropriate goals. For example, management typically wants people to set challenging goals and take risks. However, risk-taking is normally seen as something to be avoided since extremely challenging goals are likely to result in failure, which leads to punishment. Most people would rather say, "I met all my goals," even if the goals were quite easy, than say, "I missed my goals but they were extremely challenging." If you want people to set challenging goals and take risks, it may mean rewarding the person who missed all of her goals when they were extremely challenging more than the person who met all of her goals when the goals were quite easy. Show me a manager who rewards what he wants and I'll show you a successful manager. Show me one who rewards behaviors opposite to those he wants and I'll show you an unsuccessful manager.

Figure 3-2. Matrix approach to motivating people.

	Want	**Don't Want**
Getting	**Maintain**	**Decrease**
Not Getting	**Increase**	**Maintain**

The first objective of any reward system is to get people to join an organization. Thus, reward systems must, at least, be competitive with those offered by other organizations that you compete with for talent. It is unlikely that qualified candidates would join an organization that offered substantially lower starting salaries, grossly inferior benefits, and little job security. The fact that starting salaries and benefits are quite similar from company to company indicates that organizations pay a lot of attention to these factors.

Once an employee is on board, management is interested in satisfactory job performance. For many organizations, this level of performance is all that is required. If people show up on time and do the minimum required, everyone is satisfied. Reliable work that meets group norms is usually rewarded with predictable salary increases and seniority protection. Whether or not the organization is unionized, it behaves as if it is. In other organizations or with other managers, reliability is not enough. These managers would like people to perform above minimally acceptable levels. They would like them to solve problems, take initiative, exhibit teamwork, be creative, and contribute beyond their job description. This type of work environment requires rewarding individual achievement that normally results from people getting some intrinsic rewards from the work itself. It requires managers asking their people what's important to them, listening carefully, and then making every attempt to try to give people what they want, as long as it furthers the needs of the organization. For the manager, it's a never-ending bargaining and negotiation process with employees so that each employee has the opportunity to get what she perceives as important, creating a win-win situation. The rest of this chapter discusses the important theories on motivation; the following chapter details some groundbreaking research that I've conducted.

The Hawthorne Effect

For many centuries, no one worried about motivation, productivity, or a worker's feelings. You could beat people, torture them, and rub salt into their wounds. Surely, it was the golden age of management. You weren't concerned with employee turnover. When enough of them died, you just went out and captured some more. Ah, the good old days. Totally by acci-

dent, a landmark experiment was conducted that had shocking implications. In 1927, Elton Mayo, a Harvard Business School professor, led a
group of researchers at the Hawthorne Plant of the Western Electric Company in Cicero, Illinois. As reported by H. A. Landsberger (1958), they
conducted an experiment to see if increased illumination had an effect on
worker productivity. They found that it did. They then put the light back
to normal levels, but productivity increased again. They then dropped the
light to below normal levels and productivity increased again. This wasn't
the way things were supposed to go! They had the test group do a certain
amount of work per day rather than have them put in a set number of
hours. Productivity increased. They gave them a fifteen-minute break each
day. Productivity increased. They let people go home an hour early. Productivity increased. They had everyone stay an hour later. Productivity increased. Frustrated, they told the workers they were putting everything
back to normal. Productivity hit an all-time high!

It was all so baffling that this one-year study extended out to five years.
The only logical conclusion they could draw from all this was that people
liked experimenters paying attention to them. They felt needed and important. Unfortunately, by 1932, the Great Depression was in full force and
no one cared much about making people feel needed and important. The
"Hawthorne Effect" was a victim of bad timing. But the field of behavioral
science was born.

Maslow's Hierarchy of Needs

The psychologist Abraham Maslow (1954) developed a theory that has
gained wide acceptance as an explanation of human motivation. The key
concept in Maslow's theory is that there is a "hierarchy of needs." At the
lowest level are our basic biological needs, such as the need for food.
Higher-level needs, such as the need to be respected by our peers, come
into play as causes of our behavior only when lower-level needs have been
satisfied. Lower-level needs predominate until they are satisfied. Satisfying
our lower-level needs renders them inactive, and our attention then shifts
to higher-level needs.

Maslow's hierarchy recognizes five distinct levels of human needs, ar-
ranged in ascending order, as shown in Figure 3-3.

Figure 3-3. Maslow's hierarchy of needs.

1. *Survival Needs.* At the lowest level are the basic survival needs, representing a person's need for food, sleep, exercise, shelter, reproduction, and protection from the elements. People are primarily motivated by their biological drives to survive, and they will, therefore, seek work to provide sufficient income for staying alive. When these basic, first-level needs are satisfied, the person is then motivated to work toward the fulfillment of the next higher level of needs.

2. *Safety and Security.* The second level in the hierarchy is the need for safety and security. This is a need to be relatively free from danger and threats and to ensure that the basic survival needs will continue to be met in the future. In today's organizations, some security-related items are life insurance, medical insurance, short- and long-term disability, and workers compensation. For example, if a person is hurt in an accident, he is very concerned that there be some sort of salary continuance until he is able to return to work.

3. *Social Needs.* The third level is based on an individual's social needs, such as the need to belong, to associate with others, to be

accepted by peers, and to give and receive friendship and love. Many social needs are met by associations with coworkers, on and off the job. When these social needs have been adequately satisfied and the person feels accepted, then the next level of needs begins to function as the primary motivator.

4. *Ego.* The fourth level of needs—the ego needs—are related to both self-esteem and reputation. The ego needs related to self-esteem are self-confidence, independence, achievement, and job knowledge. Reputation includes the desire for status, recognition, appreciation, and the deserved respect of peers. When these fourth-level needs are satisfied, only then do the final level needs function as motivators.

5. *Self-Actualization.* The fifth level is the need for self-actualization, or the need to realize one's potential, continually develop and grow, and be creative. In short, these are the needs to become all that a person is capable of being (without joining the army). This highest level of needs is the most difficult to satisfy and tends to be meaningful only for those people who have satisfied their social and ego needs.

Herzberg's Two-Factor Theory

One of the most widely accepted theories of motivation is the "two-factor theory" developed by Frederick Herzberg (1959). He began by asking the question, "Why do people work?" Herzberg observed that people work to meet two very different sets of needs.

Herzberg called the first set of needs "maintenance needs." An individual works to satisfy the basic needs of food, shelter, clothing, security, belonging, and friendship (similar to Maslow's survival needs). The individual needs these things in almost endless amounts and is never quite satisfied with them. When these needs are met, any dissatisfaction that the person may have felt temporarily disappears. But, sooner or later, the need for more food, more clothing, etc., will arise again. These maintenance needs involve essentially the by-products of work. They have little to do with the work itself.

The other set of needs is concerned with the work itself. Long after a person has enough food, clothing, and shelter, he will persist at work, perhaps enjoying it. When asked why, the person might say something like, "It's a challenge," or "I wanted to see if I could do it," or "I've never tried to do anything like that before." If a person's job doesn't satisfy this kind of motivation need, it's likely he will seek some degree of satisfaction outside of work. There are, of course, people who don't strive to meet this need. However, the average person appears to have a need to work that has nothing to do with "maintenance" needs. The motivation need has its roots in the striving for personal growth and achievement.

Herzberg conducted a research project designed to find answers to three questions:

1. What factors cause high levels of motivation?

2. Are the factors that bring about high job satisfaction different from the factors that cause low job satisfaction or dissatisfaction?

3. What happens to people on the job as a result of changed job attitudes?

The data for Herzberg's study was obtained by detailed personal interviews with a sample of 200 engineers and accounting managers from nine companies in western Pennsylvania. The interviewee usually talked about his job, its good and bad points, using specific incidents, for several hours. Regarding the first of the questions, Herzberg found that there were ten major factors that had the most significant effect in causing attitudes to change. They are listed below, in no particular order:

• *Achievement.* Stories involving specific mention of success were put into this category. Examples were successful completion of a job, solving problems, or seeing the results of work. The definition also includes its opposite—failure or the lack of achievement.

• *Recognition.* The major criterion here was some act of recognition felt by the person. The source could be almost anyone—a manager, another member of management, a customer, a peer, or subordinates. Some act of notice, praise, or blame (negative recognition) was always involved.

- *Work Itself.* Actually doing the job, or the tasks of the job, was a source of good or bad feelings about it. Events falling into this category were related to the nature of the work and were rewarding, with or without specific achievement or recognition. Examples were creative or challenging work, varied work, or an opportunity to do a job from beginning to end.

- *Responsibility.* Individuals reported deriving satisfaction from being allowed to work without supervision, from being responsible for their own efforts, from being given responsibility for the work of others, and from being given a new kind of job duty. This category also included loss of job satisfaction stemming from a perceived lack of responsibility.

- *Advancement.* This category was used only when there was an actual change in the status or position of the person in the company (i.e., the person was promoted). In situations in which an individual transferred from one part of the company to another without a change in grade level or status but with increased opportunities for responsible work, the change was considered an increase in responsibility but not advancement.

- *Company Policy and Administration.* This category described those events in which some overall aspect of the company was a factor. There were two kinds of characteristics. One involved the adequacy or inadequacy of company organization and management. For example, there might be a situation where a person was loaned out on projects and received conflicting direction from a number of people. The person might be confused as to who the "boss" was. The consequent inefficiency, wasted duplication of effort, or struggle for power would produce frustration. The second kind of characteristic involved the beneficial or harmful effects of company policies. Personnel or financial policies, for example, might be viewed as unfair or may seem to have a detrimental effect.

- *Supervision/Technical.* This category identified events in which the critical characteristics were the competence or incompetence, fairness or unfairness of the manager. Statements about the manager's willingness or unwillingness to teach would be classified under this category. The principal consideration, however, was how well equipped the manager was to answer technical questions about the job.

- *Interpersonal Relations/Supervision.* This category involved the interpersonal relationships that arose when people interacted with their managers in the performance of their jobs. Falling into this category were statements that the manager was friendly or unfriendly, honest or dishonest, willing or unwilling to listen, or gave or withheld praise for work done.

• *Salary.* This category included events in which compensation played a role. Virtually all of these events involved wage or salary increases or unfulfilled expectations of increases. When salary occurred as a factor in low job attitudes, it tended to revolve around unfairness in the administration or perceived inadequacy of the salary increase guidelines rather than the absolute amount of the current salary. Typical problems included increases given grudgingly, increases that were late, a too-small differential between newly hired and experienced employees, and advancement not accompanied by salary increases.

• *Working Conditions.* The final category included stories where the physical conditions of work, the amount of work, or the facilities available for doing the work were mentioned. Adequacy or inadequacy of ventilation, lighting, tools, space, and other environmental characteristics were included. Complaints included inconvenience of the location of the facility, the inadequacy of tools to do the job, and the amount of work required on the job. Interestingly, workers in Herzberg's original study complained of too little work more than they complained of too much work. This is one factor that has likely changed in today's workplace.

Further analysis of the interview data provided an answer to Herzberg's second question: Are the factors that bring about high job satisfaction different from those that cause dissatisfaction or low job satisfaction? There were five factors that were rarely mentioned as producing negative job attitudes. Instead, they were mentioned most frequently when employees spoke of satisfaction with their work. Herzberg called these five factors "satisfiers." In order of frequency, they were:

1. Achievement
2. Recognition
3. Work Itself
4. Responsibility
5. Advancement

The five other factors were rarely mentioned as producing positive job attitudes. They were mentioned most frequently when employees spoke of dissatisfaction with their work. Herzberg called these factors "dissatisfiers." In order of frequency, they were:

1. Company Policy and Administration
2. Supervision/Technical
3. Salary
4. Interpersonal Relations/Supervision
5. Working Conditions

Herzberg further called our attention to a fundamental distinction between these two sets of factors. The "satisfiers" all refer to the job content: achievement of a task, recognition for task achievement, nature of the task, responsibility for the task, and professional growth or advancement in task performance. By contrast, the "dissatisfiers" refer to the job context or job environment: the nature of the company's policies and administrative practices, the type of supervision received when doing the job, the quality of the working conditions under which the job is performed, and the salary received for doing the job.

Since the dissatisfier factors describe essentially the environment and serve primarily to prevent dissatisfaction while having little effect on positive job attitudes, Herzberg referred to them as the "maintenance" factors. The satisfier factors were named the "motivators," since other findings of the study suggested that they were effective in motivating the individual to superior performance and effort.

The third question Herzberg investigated was, What happens to people on the job as a result of changed job attitudes? He looked at three general areas of "effect" and drew the following conclusions.

Performance
- In more than 60 percent of the cases studied, high attitudes resulted in high performance and low attitudes in low performance.
- Low attitudes toward the job tended to have a greater effect on performance than unfavorable ones.
- When improvement in performance was noted as a result of improved job attitudes, productivity was considerably above standard.

Turnover

- Thirteen percent of those exhibiting low attitudes quit the company within a year.
- Another 8 percent took steps toward leaving the company. They read help-wanted ads, visited employment agencies, and interviewed with other companies.
- Another 17 percent said they "thought of leaving" the company.
- Overall, during periods of low job satisfaction, 38 percent of employees withdrew from the company to some extent.

Attitudes Toward the Company

- During high job satisfaction periods, half of all employees said they had a more favorable attitude toward the company as a whole.
- Low job satisfaction led to a lower regard for the company as a place to work.
- It seems reasonable to conclude that a company may expect the degree of loyalty it gets from its employees to vary as a function of job satisfaction.

Herzberg felt the implications of the study could be summed up as an emphasis on a positive, rather than a negative, approach toward improving the "morale" of people. Few managers are resistant to the need to overcome bad maintenance conditions to avoid turnover, absenteeism, and low productivity. Herzberg didn't recommend eliminating programs aimed at improving maintenance factors. His finding supported the notion that good maintenance will prevent many of the negative results of low morale.

Yet, good maintenance should only be a beginning. An emphasis on maintenance exclusively means focusing on factors that don't really lead to job satisfaction. He felt the emphasis should be on strengthening the motivators. The rallying cry could be, "Maintenance is not enough!" Motivation to work can be strengthened by an emphasis on greater self-fulfillment. Herzberg only stated this goal and didn't present details on how it could be accomplished. That's what this book is all about.

McClelland's Social Motives

The landmark work of David McClelland (1961) on the subject of motivation may be summarized as follows:

- People have a considerable reservoir of potential energy. Studies have not indicated that differences in the total amount of potential energy are important determinants of motivation.
- All adults have a number of basic "motives" or "needs" that can be thought of as valves or outlets that channel and regulate the flow of potential energy from a person's reservoir.
- Although most adults within a given culture have the same set of motives or energy outlets, they differ greatly in the relative strength or "readiness" of various motives. A strong motive may be thought of as a valve or energy outlet that opens easily and has a larger aperture for energy flow, usually due to frequent use. A weak motive can be thought of as a tight valve that, even when open, allows only limited energy flow.

Based on this motivational model, McClelland described three intrinsic motives that have been shown to be important determinants of work-related behavior:

1. *Need for Achievement.* This is the need for personal accomplishment. A favorite phrase of someone high in this need would be, "I think I can do better." People who have high N-Ach (to use the McClelland shorthand) tend to seek out challenging or competitive situations. They also tend to take moderate risks that are under their control and will set realistic but difficult goals. There are five categories that offer clues to an individual's level of concern for achievement:

   - *Making a Unique Contribution.* The person wants to accomplish something more than an ordinary task or is observed using unique and innovative methods that will lead him to personal success.

   - *Outperforming Others.* The person engages in activities in which winning or outperforming others is a primary concern. Examples are wanting to win a race or wanting to show that you can do a better job or do it faster than others.

   - *Meeting or Surpassing a Self-Imposed Standard of Excellence.* This doesn't involve competition with others but has to do with a self-imposed standard of high quality performance. Typical examples include wanting to find a better method of doing something, working carefully on a new plan, and wanting to improve past performance.

•   *Setting Long-Term Goals.* The mere mention of a goal isn't the basis for assuming N-Ach. There must be evidence of involvement in the long-term goal (i.e., some statement of feelings about or wanting goals that lie years away).

•   *Planning to Overcome Personal and Environmental Obstacles.* High achievers carefully plan for the future by trying to anticipate any blocks to achievement of their goals. Evidence of this type of planning can be found in individuals talking about how they have overcome, or have contingency plans to overcome, barriers to goal achievement.

2.   *Need for Affiliation.* N-Aff is the motivation to be with others and to share mutual friendship. A favorite phrase of someone high in this need would be, "I really like the people I work with." Concerns of a person with the need for affiliation are:

•   *Being Part of a Group or Team.* The individual enjoys being on the "team," sacrifices her own needs for the good of the team, and enjoys the relationships and companionship that group activities can bring. Affiliation activities include parties, reunions, and recreational activities. Important events are baby showers, service anniversary dates, and birthdays.

•   *Being Liked and Accepted.* The individual talks about wanting to establish, restore, or maintain a close, warm relationship with others. This relationship is most adequately described as "friendship."

•   *Being Involved with People at Work.* The individual talks about people and working with people as the primary focus of work life.

•   *Minimizing Conflict.* Steps are taken to avoid disruptions; this person tries to smooth over uncomfortable interpersonal situations.

3. *Need for Influence.* N-Inf (sometimes called the need for power or the need for influence/power) is the motivation to exert influence or control over others. A favorite phrase of someone high in this need would be, "We crushed the competition." This person frequently uses sports and military analogies and expressions. Some clues to a person's level of need for power are:

   • *Influencing Others Through Powerful Actions.* Any forceful action serves to express this person's concern for power over others. Examples may include verbal attacks, threats, reprimands, or more subtle actions such as regulating the behavior of others through policies or giving unsolicited assistance or advice.

   • *Arousing Strong Positive or Negative Emotions in Others.* The individual exerts power by causing others to react with emotion (e.g., fear, delight, awe, or anger) to something he has purposely said or done. For a power motive to be indicated, the person's actions or words must provoke strong reactions in others and must be intended to do just that. Simply arousing other people's interest or getting their attention does not indicate a need for power.

   • *Acquiring a Reputation or Position.* This individual is concerned with public evaluation (what someone else thinks of her power). The person is concerned about reputation and other people's judgment of her powerful position. Other indicators of the power motive are whether the individual is interested in obtaining indicators of high status or shows disappointment with a perceived inferior social position.

   • *Having Control over Situations.* The individual is concerned with controlling people and situations and will seek out positions or circumstances where he can attain this kind of control.

Although any of the three social motives can be found in any organization, you would expect to have many N-Ach people in technical work such as engineering, information technology, accounting, and finance. You would expect to find many N-Aff people in helping positions such as human resources, administration, and customer service. Finally, there would be many N-Inf people in functions such as sales, marketing, and top management. The key to using this theory to your advantage is to identify which social motives are strong in different people and then to design their job to give them what they need. For example:

Social Motive	Do's	Don'ts
Achievement	Allow this person to work independently.	Ask this person to work in groups.
Affiliation	Allow this person to work cross-functionally	Ask this person to work independently.
Influence	Give this person status symbols and tokens of recognition.	Put this person in a position where the individual can't negotiate or bargain with others.

McGregor's Theory X and Theory Y

According to Douglas McGregor (1966), there are two distinct sets of assumptions about people. The assumptions lead to a consequent approach to management. The first set of assumptions, called Theory X, postulates the following:

- The average person has an inherent dislike for work and will avoid it if at all possible.
- People must be coerced, controlled, directed, and threatened with punishment to get them to put forth adequate effort.
- People prefer to be directed, wish to avoid responsibility, have little ambition, and are motivated primarily by a need for security.

Many of the assumptions in organizations that underlie traditional company rules, policies, procedures, and disciplinary action are based on Theory X. An alternative set of assumptions is called Theory Y. It states the following:

- The expenditure of physical and mental effort in work is as natural as play is to a child.
- People will exercise self-direction and self-control if committed to objectives.

- Commitment to objectives is a function of the rewards associated with their achievement.
- Under proper conditions, people will not only accept but will seek responsibility.
- People want to exercise imagination, ingenuity, and creativity in the solution of organizational problems.
- The intellectual potential of people is typically only partially utilized.

Managers who accept Theory Y push information and responsibility downward. They explain to employees the reasons why things need to be done, ask for ideas and suggestions as to how the job can be done better, and treat people the way they would like to be treated. Needless to say, the advice and actions discussed in this book are based on Theory Y assumptions.

Skinner's Positive Reinforcement Theory

B. F. Skinner (1971) described how when we do something and are rewarded, we will tend to repeat the act. In other words, the reward acts as a reinforcement. This notion is called operant conditioning, positive reinforcement, or behavior modification. The key is that by controlling the responses a person gets for his actions, the actions themselves can be controlled. Behavior modification does not probe into the reasons behind behavior.

Behavior modification first developed not as a management theory but as an outgrowth of experiments in psychology labs. These experiments represented a systematic investigation of the observation that behavior is strongly influenced by factors in the external environment. Pavlov's experiments first popularized the concept of "conditioned response." He demonstrated that when a certain stimulus (such as a bell) was associated with a reflex action (such as the appearance of food, causing a dog to salivate), the stimulus itself could eventually cause the reflex action to take place—the dog would salivate upon hearing the bell.

Skinner further refined the concept of conditioned response by dividing it into two classes—respondent (or classical) conditioning and operant conditioning. Respondent conditioning can be thought of as involuntary, such as the reflexes of Pavlov's dogs. Conversely, operant conditioning consists of voluntary behaviors that are influenced by the consequences that follow and reinforce them. In operant conditioning, all that is required for a subject to perform an action is the subject's estimation that a desired response will occur.

While negative reinforcement and ignoring a behavior may successfully halt unwanted behavior, a number of undesirable side effects may be generated. Tension is created under conditions of punishment. The person punished often develops feelings of hostility and aggression. The net effect is usually to make the situation worse. Ignoring a problem causes fewer side effects but has many of the same limitations. It can only control unwanted behavior and cannot replace it with something more productive. Thus, Skinner felt that positive reinforcement achieves the best long-term results, and behavior modification programs rely on its use.

Positive reinforcement can take many forms including money, recognition, time off from the job, and praise. In addition, there are several other important ideas related to the concept of reinforcement:

- *If one behavior is asked for and a second behavior is reinforced, the second behavior will tend to be repeated.* Despite all of the management speeches and policy statements, whatever behavior is really rewarded will tend to be repeated.
- *If behavior is not useful on the job or has no consequence when it occurs, it will tend to stop occurring.* Unrewarded actions are extinguished over time.
- *The further removed in time a consequence is from an action, the less effect that consequence will have on the action.* Rewards should follow the behavior closely in order to have full impact as reinforcement.

Positive reinforcement is an ongoing process wherein a manager systematically reinforces the positive aspects of the employee's performance. Managers should provide recognition that neither exaggerates nor undervalues the importance of an employee's contributions.

Vroom's Expectancy Theory

Originally developed by Victor Vroom (1964), expectancy theory is based on the combination of three variables—effort, performance, and rewards. These variables, as shown in Figure 3-4, are defined in the following way:

1. *Effort-performance (E-P) expectancies* are the extent to which the person believes that trying will lead to high performance.

2. *Performance-reward (P-R) expectancies* are the extent to which a person believes that high performance will lead to desired rewards.

3. *Value of the reward* refers to the attractiveness of the rewards the person receives for performance. This depends, for the most part, on the unsatisfied needs of the individual. In other words, a dollar might be very important to a homeless person but be seen as something of little value to a millionaire.

Expectancy theory gives strong consideration to needs, since the performance-reward expectancy depends on meeting important, unsatisfied needs. Expectancy theory points out that motivation is heavily dependent on the actions the manager takes. The more the manager can do to clarify the two expectancies for employees, the higher their motivation level should be. The attractiveness of the rewards to each person must be considered. For one person, the opportunity to attend conferences and trade shows might be critically important, while for another person it may be seen as a burden.

Figure 3-4. Effort, performance, and rewards: expectations and outcomes.

Adams's Equity Theory

"Equity" is the idea that the value of what a person puts into the job and satisfaction he gets from it are largely determined by comparisons to others. Equity theory, developed by J. Stacy Adams (1965), formalized these relationships. Adams's model (as displayed in Figure 3-5) says that a person's ratio of job inputs to job outcomes is compared to the ratio for other people in similar situations. When the ratios are about the same, people tend to be satisfied with the rewards they received. When the ratios are different, they usually take action to bring them back into balance. For example, if you feel you aren't being paid enough relative to other people, you might cut back on how hard you work. Or you might start coming in late and leaving early. On the other hand, if you feel you're being overpaid, the resultant guilt might cause you to work harder or longer hours.

There are two important points that follow from these equity ideas. First, relative rewards are as important as their absolute amounts. Second, management must take these equity comparisons into account when giving rewards. This doesn't mean that everyone should get the same rewards. It means that high performance must be consistently rewarded if it is expected to continue. It also means that poor performance shouldn't be rewarded if the high performers are to feel satisfied.

Figure 3-5. Equity theory.

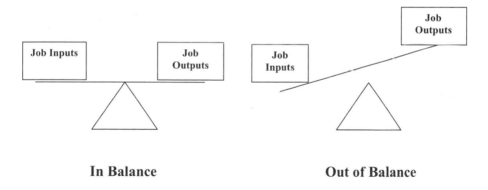

In Balance   **Out of Balance**

Conclusions from the Popular Theories of Motivation

Managers can do much to provide a climate conducive to job satisfaction where the individual's needs can be met. The two dimensions of a conducive work environment are:

1. The nature of the job the person is doing (e.g., routine or monotonous, challenging or lacking challenge).

2. The way the manager manages (i.e., the amount of freedom she allows, the amount of praise and recognition she gives).

The popular theories of motivation are not in conflict with one another. They seem to all agree that each person has his own needs that must be satisfied if he is going to put forth an above-average effort, and that an individual's needs can vary over time. Taken together, these different theories of motivation also suggest some guidelines for the manager who wants to motivate people to better work performance:

• *People have reasons for doing what they do.* People are goal-oriented. Behavior tends to be directed toward a reward. If you want to know why a person behaves a certain way, you have to know what that person sees as the benefit of behaving that way. Behavior doesn't occur in a vacuum or randomly. People have needs, and they work to fulfill them.

• *People choose a course of action or make a decision that gives results that have value to them.* People choose to work in a way that will get them what they want most. They're looking for some kind of goal or reward. The manager can influence behavior by making the "right" rewards available to a certain person.

• *Faced with a reward that is easily attainable and one that is less so, people tend to choose the reward that is more easily attainable.* People usually opt for caution over daring. A person may want the reward that goes with deciding on course of action "A." If the outcome of the effort is uncertain, however, the person may well choose course of action "B." Even though the value of the latter is not as significant, the outcome may be more predictable. When assigning a project, asking someone to take on a new job, or helping a subordinate plot a career path, it's essential to keep in mind that the value of a course of action is only one factor. The question the employee is probably asking is, "What are my chances of succeeding?" Is it worth the effort to try? That's the more important consideration to an employee. Managers can take steps to bolster people's perception that the chances of success are worth the effort.

Many managers have difficulty in getting employees to work better, smarter, and with higher quality results because they fail to see the situation through the eyes of the employee. They say, "I need you to do this right away," or "Can you do me a favor?" or "You're really going to enjoy this assignment." They assume that their employees should feel the same way they do. It's just like the managers who couldn't define "motivation" because their assumptions centered on themselves, not their employees. Managers would do well to take into account the employee's viewpoint. As Skinner demonstrated, if you let people know exactly what you expect of them and then reward them for doing it, you're very likely to get a repetition of good performance. At the very least, you're more likely to get repeated performance if you reward than if you do not.

What often happens in reality? Managers get busy and distracted. They reward on an intermittent, sporadic basis. They fail, through their inconsistency, to convey the all-important message to employees: "If you work effectively for me, I'll make it worth your while." People want certain things from work. Many employees feel it's owed to them. The manager who forgets these facts of working life, or refuses to accept them, risks getting mediocre employee performance.

What People Really Want

As you saw from the discussion of motivation theory in Chapter 3, the classic literature discussed "employees" without differentiating between levels. I was curious to find out if there were any differences between nonexempt employees, exempt professionals, and managers. The research discussed in this chapter involved asking people directly what their needs are in a job and to what extent those needs were being satisfied. In addition, they were asked what their needs are in a relationship with their manager and to what extent those needs were being satisfied. Then I examined whether there are differences between people in various levels of an organization. It is common for people to blame other levels and say, "They don't understand us," or "I don't understand them," or "All they care about is themselves." Three distinct groups of people were examined for their feelings on job satisfaction and satisfaction with their manager. This research included interviews with members of management, exempt professionals, and nonexempt employees and sought to answer several key questions. Are they the same? Are they different? If they're different, what are those differences?

During the first half of 2006, I conducted a research study in twenty-five organizations in the United States. A total of 813 people were asked to rank-order the importance of twenty elements of job satisfaction, with a rating of "1" being given to the highest element. They were then asked to rate their satisfaction with each element on a scale of 1 to 5, with "5" being the highest level of satisfaction. They were also asked to rate their overall satisfaction with the job itself. A section of the questionnaire was also devoted to satisfaction with the boss. Respondents were asked to rank-order the importance of ten elements of satisfaction, with a "1" being given to the highest element. They were then asked to rate, on a 1 to 5 scale, their satisfaction with each element, with "5" being the highest level of satisfaction. They were also asked to rate their overall satisfaction with the boss.

The job satisfaction elements chosen were the same as the "system outcomes" used by Richard Huseman and John Hatfield (1989). The elements for satisfaction with the boss were similar to the eleven "management strategies" they described to improve an employee's perception of job equity. Huseman and Hatfield used four strategies—"negative feedback," "participation," "criticism," and "novel rewarding behaviors"—that I replaced with "constructive criticism," "input into decisions," and "development activities." The participants in the study were attending company-sponsored training programs. There is no reason to believe the samples were not representative of others in those organizations. They were also left on their own to define the elements. If I was asked what a word or phrase meant, I responded by saying, "Answer on the basis of what that word or phrase means to you." The complete survey is reproduced here.

Job Satisfaction Survey

	Rank order of importance to me in my job (1–20, with 1 the highest)	Satisfaction rating (1–5, with 5 the highest)
Sense of accomplishment	_____	_____
Recognition for good work	_____	_____
Doing challenging work	_____	_____
Pay	_____	_____
Sense of competence	_____	_____
Status	_____	_____
Making use of my abilities	_____	_____
Fringe benefits	_____	_____
Feeling of personal worth	_____	_____
Feeling of belonging	_____	_____
Making decisions	_____	_____

Promotion and advancement	_____	_____
Feeling of achievement	_____	_____
Appreciation from others	_____	_____
Having responsibility	_____	_____
Job security	_____	_____
Sense of confidence	_____	_____
Friendships on the job	_____	_____
Doing meaningful work	_____	_____
Working conditions	_____	_____

Overall satisfaction with the job   _____

	Rank order of importance to me in my boss (1–10, with 1 the highest)	Satisfaction rating (1–5, with 5 the highest)
Positive expectations	_____	_____
Goal-setting	_____	_____
Positive feedback	_____	_____
Availability	_____	_____
Trust	_____	_____
Constructive criticism	_____	_____
Providing information	_____	_____
Input into decisions	_____	_____
Development activities	_____	_____
Two-way communication	_____	_____

Overall satisfaction with my boss   _____

Nonexempt _____   Exempt Professional _____   Manager _____

Terminology Used in Analysis

The following definitions will be used in the analysis of the Job Satisfaction Survey results:

Rank Order of Importance

Rating	Importance in Job	Importance in Boss
"Critical"	Top 5 Factors	Top 3 Factors
"Very Important"	Next 5 Factors	Next 2 Factors
"Somewhat Important"	Next 5 Factors	Next 2 Factors
"Least Important"	Last 5 Factors	Last 3 Factors

Satisfaction

Rating	Point Total
"Extremely Well Met"	4.00 +
"Well Met"	3.50–3.99

"Somewhat Met"	3.00–3.49
"Unmet"	Below 3.00

Overall Job Satisfaction Survey Results
(N = 813)

	Rank order of importance to me in my job (1–20, with 1 the highest)	Satisfaction rating (1–5, with 5 the highest)
Sense of accomplishment	4.16	3.82
Recognition for good work	7.36	3.21
Doing challenging work	6.08	3.55
Pay	8.46	3.28
Sense of competence	9.24	3.92
Status	15.38	3.12
Making use of my abilities	7.64	3.37
Fringe benefits	13.82	3.41
Feeling of personal worth	8.89	3.77
Feeling of belonging	14.00	3.59
Making decisions	12.57	3.30
Promotion and advancement	9.67	3.00
Feeling of achievement	7.51	3.57
Appreciation from others	12.20	3.55
Having responsibility	10.14	3.73
Job security	11.52	3.31
Sense of confidence	10.29	3.92
Friendships on the job	16.50	3.66
Doing meaningful work	9.54	3.62
Working conditions	15.80	3.56
Overall satisfaction with the job		3.64

	Rank order of importance to me in my boss (1–10, with 1 the highest)	Satisfaction rating (1–5, with 5 the highest)
Positive expectations	4.69	3.50
Goal-setting	5.72	2.95
Positive feedback	3.61	3.07
Availability	7.05	3.43
Trust	3.34	3.68
Constructive criticism	7.87	3.06
Providing information	5.43	3.31
Input into decisions	6.13	3.13

Development activities	7.21	2.90
Two-way communication	3.95	3.35
Overall satisfaction with my boss		3.41

Analysis of Overall Results

"Importance to Me in My Job," Ranked by Order of Importance
1. "Sense of accomplishment"—Critical, well met
2. "Doing challenging work"—Critical, well met
3. "Recognition for good work"—Critical, somewhat met
4. "Feeling of achievement"—Critical, well met
5. "Making use of my abilities"—Critical, somewhat met
6. "Pay"—Very important, somewhat met
7. "Feeling of personal worth"—Very important, well met
8. "Sense of competence"—Very important, well met
9. "Doing meaningful work"—Very important, well met
10. "Promotion and advancement"—Very important, somewhat met
11. "Having responsibility"—Somewhat important, somewhat met
12. "Sense of confidence"—Somewhat important, well met
13. "Job security"—Somewhat important, somewhat met
14. "Appreciation from others"—Somewhat important, well met
15. "Making decisions"—Somewhat important, somewhat met
16. "Fringe benefits"—Least important, somewhat met
17. "Sense of belonging"—Least important, well met
18. "Working conditions"—Least important, well met
19. "Status"—Least important, somewhat met
20. "Friendships on the job"—Least important, well met

"Importance to Me in My Boss," Ranked by Order of Importance
1. "Trust"—Critical, well met
2. "Positive feedback"—Critical, somewhat met
3. "Two-way communication"—Critical, somewhat met
4. "Positive expectations"—Very important, well met
5. "Providing information"—Very important, somewhat met
6. "Goal-setting"—Somewhat important, unmet
7. "Input into decisions"—Somewhat important, somewhat met
8. "Availability"—Least important, somewhat met
9. "Development activities"—Least important, unmet
10. "Constructive criticism"—Least important, somewhat met

Overall Satisfaction Scores

*"Satisfaction with the job itself"—Well met
*"Satisfaction with my boss"—Somewhat met

Summary of Survey Results

The complete breakdown of the results for nonexempts, exempt professionals, and managers is shown in the Appendix. Overall, the survey revealed remarkable similarities in terms of what these three groups wanted from a job and from a boss.

Critical or "Empowerment" Factors

The critical factors were virtually identical, except for pay, which was third on the nonexempt list but did not appear on either the exempt professional or manager list. This is likely due to the fact that the nonexempt group is the lowest paid. Something becomes more important to a person who doesn't have much of it.

Importance in Job

Nonexempt	Exempt Professional	Manager
Accomplishment	Accomplishment	Accomplishment
Pay	Challenge	Challenge
Challenge	Achievement	Recognition
Use abilities	Recognition	Use abilities
Recognition	Use abilities	Achievement

Importance in Boss

Nonexempt	Exempt Professional	Manager
Positive feedback	Positive feedback	Trust
Trust	Trust	Two-way communication
Two-way communication	Two-way communication	Positive feedback

The critical items fit together. They're a set. They represent a roadmap for the things a manager should do to increase job satisfaction. They're the higher-level needs on Maslow's hierarchy. They are Herzberg's motivation factors. They are what I like to call the "empowerment factors." They are key to a manager getting extraordinary results from ordinary people.

Least Important Factors

The critical items were distinctly different from the least important factors, which were also virtually identical for all three groups.

Importance in Job

Nonexempt	*Exempt Professional*	*Manager*
Making decisions	Sense of belonging	Fringe benefits
Working conditions	Friendships	Sense of belonging
Sense of belonging	Status	Status
Friendships	Fringe benefits	Working conditions
Status	Working conditions	Friendships

Importance in Boss

Nonexempt	*Exempt Professional*	*Manager*
Availability	Development activities	Availability
Development activities	Availability	Constructive criticism
Constructive criticism	Constructive criticism	Development activities

These least important items fit together also. They are extrinsic or outside the job. They are like the lower-level needs in Maslow's hierarchy, Herzberg's maintenance factors, or what I like to call the "traditional" factors, since they are the things that managers through the years have typically concentrated on providing for their employees. They were likely important to the 813 people who responded to the Job Satisfaction Survey, but nowhere near as important as the "empowerment" factors.

Increasing Job Satisfaction

There are "right questions" that you, as the manager, can ask employees so that they can tell you what it will take to give them more job satisfaction and satisfaction with you. The ones listed here aren't the only appropriate questions, but they are representative questions. Most employees don't volunteer this type of information. They'd really appreciate being asked.

Job Satisfaction Questions

- What can be done to give you a greater feeling of responsibility and control?
- What happens *before* you get an assignment that might be included in the assignment (e.g., budgeting, formulating a project plan, determining the need, getting approvals, etc.)?
- What happens *after* you finish an assignment that might be included in the assignment (e.g., evaluating results, summarizing accomplishments, presenting results to management, etc.)?

- Can larger segments of the job be given to you? What is it that you want to do that you're not doing now?
- What things could be added to the job for you to learn? What problems would you like to be given to solve?
- What are *you* doing that another employee could do or be taught to do?
- When someone leaves the organization, would you want to take over part of that job?
- Can you do more of the determining of due dates, priorities, and day-to-day scheduling?
- Can performance measurements be made available directly to you?
- How can you be given more authority? Do you have to check too many things with me or others?
- What do I do for you that you could do for yourself?
- What responsibility could you assume when I'm on vacation, traveling on business, in a training program, or otherwise unavailable?
- On what decisions could your advice and recommendations be sought?
- What new things do you want to learn? In turn, is there training that you could give to others in the organization?
- What am I doing that's irritating or frustrating for you?
- Can your skills be highlighted more? Do others see you as the expert they should contact directly with a particular type of problem?
- How are your achievements recognized? Can this recognition be made more meaningful? Do you feel appreciated by me and others?

Employees crave the "empowerment" factors, but managers often feel uncomfortable in providing them. Here are some ways that managers can get the most impact from a reward, for example:

- *Tailor the reward to the person.* Shy people, for example, aren't going to feel very good making speeches in front of your organization. Give them assignments that mean something to them.
- *Time the recognition as close as possible to the event.* Delaying can weaken the impact and actually produce a negative response. Imagine how

an employee would react to a statement such as, "I really like that recommendation you made eleven years ago. I've been meaning to say something to you about it."

• *Make sure employees know specifically what they are being recognized for.* Putting someone's name on a generic Employee of the Month plaque often defeats the purpose of showing appreciation for someone's specific contribution.

• *Be creative in using reward techniques.* Things that are unexpected and not done out of any sense of obligation tend to be the most appreciated. Sending an e-greeting card with animation and music can show sincerity in giving praise. You've committed the praise to writing.

• *Give people something they value in the way of additional responsibility.* A manager shows he genuinely appreciates employees when he gives them something lasting—trust. It says, "You've earned the freedom to make more of a contribution. You're important to me and I want to demonstrate that fact to you."

Steps for Empowering Employees

Empowerment is created when managers ask their people what they want and do their best to give it to them. Stating what they want is essential if employees are going to take responsibility for their own job satisfaction. The following are some specific steps that managers can take to help empower employees:

• *Stay focused on what people want.* This is particularly helpful when people get caught up in complaining, blaming others, and exhibiting defensive behavior. Asking "What do you want?" helps turn things toward specific actions.

• *Engage in acts that give others ownership.* People commit to that which they own. Managers create ownership and build commitment when they give employees some measure of freedom to choose their own path to achieving results. Decisions made by management are often resented. The very same decisions made after a recommendation by employees tend to be welcomed, with management being viewed as "responsive" and "caring."

• *Confront passive behavior.* Often, nonassertive behavior is a form of aggression. Passive people frequently remain silent as a strategy for getting revenge. They remove their energy, effort, and enthusiasm from a situation. It's usually best for the manager to encourage people by letting them know they have a lot to offer. As manager, you need their full contribution for group success. Then, it's extremely important to thank them after they deliver what you've asked for.

• *Create a vision for the future.* People respond to those who have a clear, compelling idea of how they want things to be. Work brings out the best in people when a vision is defined and they commit to overcoming whatever obstacles might be in the way of making that vision a reality.

Money is a wonderful reward. Under Theory X assumptions, it's the most important motivator because people work primarily for economic reasons. Under Theory Y assumptions, you need to offer more than money to motivate people. Money is often seen by employees as an easy way out for the manager. When giving a monetary reward, make it a meaningful and personal event as opposed to awkwardly handing it out without explanation. "Pay" was the sixth highest job satisfaction overall and the second most important item among nonexempt employees, according to the survey findings. It's a multifaceted incentive, having both economic and psychological meaning. In addition to providing for physical and safety needs, it also helps to satisfy such needs as power, status, self-esteem, recognition, and sense of achievement. How a person compares in compensation with those he sees as equals may be more important than the amount of money he earns. Money, then, is certainly an important factor in job satisfaction, although not at the top of the scale. A good way to look at it is that if people are underpaid, they'll be dissatisfied. However, if they're paid competitively, you'll need more than money to fully satisfy them. Furthermore, it's debatable as to whether giving additional amounts of money leads to higher levels of satisfaction.

The ideas that follow represent additional examples of the kinds of things managers can do to increase job satisfaction. The outstanding manager learns through experience which combination of approaches works best for each employee. With tasks that need to be done in a group, most managers ask, "Who's the best person to do this job?" They should also ask, "Is there an opportunity to give someone additional job satisfaction?" If you want to give your people increased job satisfaction, consider doing the following:

• *Remove some controls while retaining accountability.* Give employees freedom to pursue tasks in their own way while establishing agreed-upon results and standards of performance.

• *Increase the accountability of people for their own work.* Encourage an active role on the part of employees in defining, implementing, and communicating progress on tasks.

• *Give people a complete natural unit of work.* Entrust employees with completion of whole projects whenever possible, or at least explain the task's relevance to larger projects or overall goals.

• *Grant additional authority to employees in their activities.* Give them the ability to accomplish meaningful tasks using their own methods.

• *Make periodic reports directly available to the employees.* Give them access to information that in the past might have been available only to the manager.

• *Introduce new and more difficult tasks.* Assign work that challenges people. Be sure they're provided with the training and guidance necessary to successfully complete the tasks.

• *Assign people specialized tasks that allow them to build their expertise.* Give them work based on needs and interests, and consider whether the employee will see the responsibility as a benefit.

• *Give people the recognition they deserve.* Most people who accomplish something significant like that fact to be known. The manager can mention it to higher management, put a special commendation on the department's website, have an article written in the company newspaper, or simply call for a round of applause at a department conference call.

• *Grant more freedom to do the job.* Employees may be given the chance to set their own work hours or to work at home. Other employees could be permitted to review their own work instead of having it checked by someone else.

- *Allow employees the opportunity to represent you.* A valuable employee could chair a meeting for you or take that business trip that you normally would take. At the very least, when you have lunch with an important customer or vendor, you can invite that key performer along with you.

- *Have employees attend higher-level meetings.* Merely sitting in as a bystander at regularly scheduled operating meetings can be an important learning experience and add breadth to someone's understanding of the organization.

- *Have them serve as an instructor or conference leader.* People asked to prepare and present material often say they learn more about the topic than the people who attend. The role of expert requires the person to make an in-depth exploration of the subject matter.

- *Redesign a job.* Change the content of a job to build in opportunities for the employee to utilize a wider repertoire of her skills and abilities.

- *Give replacement assignments.* When you or someone else is traveling or on vacation, give employees the chance to play a temporary role. It really helps if you can let others know this person has full signing authority.

- *Have them represent you.* Ask employees to attend meetings with the understanding that they are speaking on your behalf. A side benefit is that it frees up some time for you to do other aspects of your job.

- *Give them more work.* Not in quantity necessarily, but more challenging, interesting, responsible, and rewarding work. You might consider delegating a task that you prize. Be sure to explain your intentions. You're giving employees a richer assignment because they have done so well.

- *Give them training.* Unfortunately, for many organizations, training has the negative connotation, someone is "deficient and therefore needs training." Instead, have employees attend training as part of their development. It can broaden their perspective, offer new insights, and deepen the thinking of participants. Some companies are smart enough to take this a step further and "nominate" people who have earned the right to attend the development program for high-potential people.

- *Give them more of you.* I don't mean offering closer supervision, of course. The good employee deserves less supervision, not more. Rather, make yourself or another respected person available on a less formal mentoring basis. Exchange ideas with your employees. Maybe they could use some career counseling. Remember, the number-one thing employees want from their manager is "trust." Do some things that will build a trusting relationship.

• *Play favorites.* Don't be afraid to recognize top performers. The people who do the best job should receive more of your attention. The message should be, "This is what I do for people who perform well. If you perform well, you'll get these favors, too." That kind of favoritism works in the manager's advantage.

Delegating Effectively

Empowerment and delegation allow managers to release themselves to do other tasks, enrich the employee's job, and provide opportunity for increased job satisfaction. Essentially, what's sound delegation for the manager can be seen as empowerment by the employee.

Delegation is a way to communicate positive feedback to employees. The very act of delegating tasks shows that managers trust their employees, respect their skills, and have confidence in their abilities and potential for greater contribution to the organization. Effective delegation processes build in feedback points as progress on the assignment is communicated by the employee to the manager. This communication should be two-way, encouraging the exchange of ideas. There are, unfortunately, a number of reasons why delegation has a bad name and is underutilized as a development tool. Delegation is often seen as a manager "dumping" work on people that the manager doesn't want to do. In such cases, delegation is resented and people believe the manager is taking advantage of them.

Delegation may trigger feelings of loss in the manager—loss of power, loss of authority, loss of achievement, and loss of control. The delegation process is often seen by the manager as subtractive (i.e., the job delegated is taken away from the manager) rather than additive (i.e., the delegated job increases the employee's job satisfaction and helps the employee to prepare for advancement). Even if managers accept the necessity of developing employees and understand the role that delegation can play in the process, development of employees may not be a behavior that's rewarded by the organization. Given a low organizational priority, employee development may have to wait until the myriad daily tasks have been attended to. In other words, it will never happen.

Effective delegation, whether for the purpose of developing employees or for other reasons, is not easy. It requires the ability to plan, organize, and control many activities with specific goals and instruction. As such, delegation cannot be expected to come easily or naturally. Unless managers understand the delegation process and dedicate themselves to it, employee job satisfaction and satisfaction with the manager will likely remain around a 3.0 or 3.5 on a five-point scale—acceptable but certainly not world-class.

Action Items for Developing Your Ability to Motivate Others

Motivating Others—Demonstrating a focused approach to managing people that emphasizes setting expectations in a compelling manner, measuring and evaluating results, giving feedback, and acknowledging or recognizing appropriate outcomes.

• Demonstrate your personal commitment to the department and your staff and praise commitment demonstrated by *them*.

• When you assign new projects, take the time to explain how they fit in with overall department objectives. When employees understand how their work contributes to the whole, their commitment tends to increase.

• Make it a point to regularly reinforce the importance of each person's contributions and the worker's value to overall department objectives.

• Create a high-performance environment where:
  • The focus is clear.
  • The work is challenging.
  • People feel appreciated.
  • Barriers to accomplishing work are kept to a minimum.
  • Resources are available.
  • People help and support each other.

• Identify your employees' perception of how things can be better tomorrow than they are today. Ask them the following types of questions to gain a clearer understanding of your current environment and what needs to be done to make it more conducive to high performance:

- What have you done recently that you're most proud of?
- What gives you the most job satisfaction?
- What kinds of challenges would you like to take on in the future?
- What obstacles exist to doing your work?
- What resources are available to you? What resources are not available that you'd like to have?

- List the needs and corresponding rewards you believe to be most relevant to each employee, based on your knowledge of the person.

- Initiate a discussion with each employee to learn, directly from the source, what that person perceives her needs to be. Compare the list supplied by the employee with the list of your perceptions to determine your level of understanding.

- Observe employees over time and add to or alter the list of needs. For example, you would change the list if you discovered that people did not mention certain needs because they would be embarrassed (e.g., someone might not want to admit that he craves frequent recognition). Conversely, someone might indicate he is interested in advancement even though that's not true. To say otherwise, that person reasons, would be to show lack of ambition.

- Observe employees to determine the optimum timing for rewards. Some employees may respond best to frequent encouragement and recognition throughout a project while others may respond best to receiving rewards upon project completion.

- Seek feedback on your motivational abilities from peers skilled in this area. If appropriate, arrange for coaching to improve your skills. Observe skilled motivators in action and incorporate their approaches.

- Add new tasks to the employee's job to widen the variety of skills used in performing the job. This practice can increase motivation by reducing boredom.

- Increase your employees' authority and accountability. Give them full decision-making responsibility in areas where your approval was formerly required.

• Increase your employees' visibility. For example, an employee who formerly prepared reports for your signature might now submit them under his own name, or someone who prepared a presentation for you to give might now give the presentation.

• Give employees the opportunity to attend conferences or meetings as the company or department representative.

• Increase the meaningfulness of assigned tasks. An employee who previously completed only a portion of a task might be permitted to handle the entire task alone or with others, to have the satisfaction of producing a total product.

• Increase the amount of feedback on performance. Feedback can come from you or from the employees themselves. For example, a technician can keep a tally of the number of "callback" service calls received on equipment services, conduct a monthly analysis, and recommend actions to be taken.

• Periodically assign special projects that you otherwise would have taken on yourself, to provide challenge and visibility to employees instead.

Attracting and Retaining
Top Talent

Interviewing: Choosing the Best from the Rest

Most employee performance problems can be traced back to the hiring process. When a manager points a finger at employees and says, "They didn't work out," most of the time there are three fingers pointing back at the manager. The reason is usually "because you should never have hired the person in the first place." The "you" may have been the manager before you or the manager before that. But a hiring mistake was probably made. Why criticize the employee when we (management) put the wrong person in the wrong job? That doesn't seem fair.

A lot of managers don't give the interviewing process the time and attention it deserves. If you say, "I just need a warm body," then that's probably just what you're going to get (and what you deserve). Bringing aboard a permanent employee is more expensive than most people would imagine. For instance:

- You hire a programmer who earns $50,000 a year and works for ten years.
- You mark up the base salary by a conservative 35 percent for benefits and another 35 percent for overhead expenses.

- You give the person a combined 5 percent a year in merit and promotional increases.
- The total is over $1 million!

Think of the other million-dollar decisions or recommendations you make. I'll bet you give them a lot of time and attention. I'll bet you have to do your research and analysis. I'll bet you have to defend your recommendations. Interviewing job candidates should be the same way. If you don't have an outstanding candidate, don't fill the job. Keep on looking. It's better to leave a requisition open than to hire someone who'll negatively impact your department. One poor or mediocre person in an otherwise good group can sabotage the morale of the entire group. If you don't have an outstanding candidate, get the work done some other way. Use consultants, contractors, temporary workers, or any other creative thing you can think of. Just don't fill the job. You'll pay the price later.

Avoid Common Mistakes

Many managers, unfortunately, select people based on how well they interview. In other words, someone who is glib, articulate, and well prepared tends to be the one who gets the job. Many managers say things like, "I'm very impressed with a candidate who has been on our website and has researched the company." They often say, "I like this candidate because he has five years of experience. The others don't have any more than three." Or they say, "She answered some tough questions very well." You know what? How well someone interviews, how much preparation they've done, or how many years of experience they have is all irrelevant. They aren't useful factors. That doesn't mean, of course, that you want to hire someone who interviews terribly, is totally unprepared, and doesn't have the relevant experience. What you *do* want is someone who has shown a track record of success. Someone who knows how to get things done. Someone who is a good fit for the job. If someone has five years of failing, that's not as good as three years of succeeding on the job.

So, forget if someone is "Our kind of guy" or "Has the right chemistry with me" or "Would fit in well around here." Some of the most successful people I've known, particularly technical people, weren't "our kind of guy" at all and didn't have much "chemistry" and didn't necessarily "fit in well." You wouldn't hire a surgeon to operate on you because he is a nice person, a good corporate citizen, or everyone's friend. You should be hiring people because, based on their track record, there is strong evidence that they will be successful in the job you want them to do.

I remember a software manager who came to me and said there was a senior programmer his management was complaining about: "The director and the vice president don't like the fact that he sits and stares out the window a lot of the time. They don't think he's working." I asked how good the programmer was. "He's brilliant," said the manager. "He comes up with software solutions that no one else could. So what should I do?" I replied, "Buy him a bigger window!" It's like having a job opening for a physicist and not hiring Albert Einstein because you don't like someone who wears mismatched socks. Hire Einstein! Who cares about his socks?

Suppose you had money to invest in a golfer. Would you choose the golfer on the basis of who interviews the best or knows the most theory about how to hit a golf ball? I'd sponsor Tiger Woods. Why? He knows how to win golf tournaments. Pure and simple. I don't care how he does it or why he does it or what motivates him. I don't have to be an amateur psychologist and try to figure him out. Those things don't matter. Keep it plain and simple. He knows how to win golf tournaments. That's all that matters. He has a good track record of doing the things you want him to do.

In fact, it's literally like a "track record." If you and I as amateurs went to the racetrack, we'd bet on horses based on irrelevant things. We don't know any better. We'd bet on horse number 5 because five is our lucky number. We'd bet on the prettiest horse. Or the one who looks the fastest. Or the one with the funniest name or the most attractive silks. Once in a while, we'd win. But over the course of the night, the odds are that we'd wind up losing. A professional gambler does it differently. He looks at the factors that lead to success. Things like breeding, track conditions, experience with this kind of track and this kind of distance, who the horse has run against in the past, the horse's experience with this particular jockey, and how many races the horse has won against what kind of competition.

It's objective. It's factual. The gambler doesn't care if the horse speaks well, is a good citizen, or has checked out racing websites. The gambler raises his chances of a successful bet by doing what managers should do—paying attention to track record. Of particular interest is the *recent* track record. If the professional gambler can get inside information on how the horse is feeling today and how the horse ran in this morning's workout, so much the better.

So, don't be thrown by appearances and your personal biases. If a horse has won its last five races, I'd be hard pressed to bet against it. If a horse has finished last in every race, I really don't care how many years of experience it has, how much preparation it has done, or whether it talks a good game. I'm not likely to bet on it. And you shouldn't, either. Don't ever think that candidate with many years of bumbling around is a better hire than someone with a few years of great accomplishment. Yet, amazingly, many managers would choose the candidate with the most years of experience.

An effective line of questioning is to ask about "lessons learned." Good people (like us) are constantly improving. We take something and make it better. Bad people (the kind you don't want to hire) accept things as they are. For example, if someone conducted a new employee orientation, ask about how he or she improved the program. The good person will say, "Based on input from the people we put through the program and the hiring managers, I tweaked this and modified that," and will tell you how the program got better and better. A bad person will respond with, "Huh? What do you mean?"—not even understanding the question. For bad people, work is about doing what they're told. They don't think in terms of improving themselves or putting anything of themselves into the projects, tasks, and assignments they're given. If things go wrong, they'll just blame someone else. "That's the way I was told to do it" will be their likely response. Their level in the organization or the type of organization has nothing to do with it. Their development is like a "flat line." As in a hospital, the flat-liners are brain dead. I'll always take someone whose development has been like a skyrocket over someone who has many years of experience as a flat-liner. Flat-liners' experience isn't really worth much.

Look for Someone Who Has Done the Things That Lead to Job Success

If you're not sure what the key job requirements are, talk to job incumbents. Choose the best people. Make it a focus group of the top performers. They'll help you. It's in their best interest to help. They want you to hire a strong performer because it'll make their job easier. Ask them what the key determinants of success are and what they all have in common. Or simply look at the resumes or applications of the top performers. Compare them with resumes or applications of the bottom performers. Try to figure out what to look for and what to avoid. A little bit of analysis can save you some recruiting nightmares.

The hires I'm proudest of through the years are those that seemed off-target and out-of-the-ordinary. For example, I remember getting a requisition for a customer call center manager that listed all the technical things this person had to know about telephones and computers. I went out and got someone who was in charge of a ski resort. The director didn't even want to interview the person. I persisted and said this person had transferable skills, was brilliant at handling customer issues and motivating staff, and would learn the technical aspects of the job in no time. The director reluctantly interviewed the candidate. He loved him. He was hired and went on to become a senior vice president. The candidates who were a little off-center and required some selling are the ones I'm proudest of. Maybe because it took some imagination to be able to see their transferable skills.

It's easy to be impressed with someone who says, "I'm a take-charge person who really responds to a challenge." The key is to use a statement like that as a starting point. It's a good answer but it's a textbook, rehearsed answer. It doesn't mean that the candidate is good. It doesn't mean that the candidate is bad. That's the way most people talk during an interview and they usually are allowed to get away with it. What you need to do next is say, "Can you give me an example of something you really took charge of?" Or maybe, "What was the biggest challenge you've responded to recently?" Don't ask questions that allow someone to give you theoretical responses. Don't ask things like, "Can you tell me what your strengths and weaknesses are?" or "Can you describe yourself in one word?" or "If you were an animal, what kind of animal would you be?" Instead look for specific examples of what someone has accomplished.

Another useful technique is to ask questions that give negative information. In other words, after asking about a successful experience, ask for a failure experience. You'll typically learn more about a job candidate by the things she tried to do but failed at. You could ask, "Tell me about an idea you sold to management," and then follow it with, "Tell me about an idea you tried to sell to management but couldn't." Don't only use the negative question by itself because it sounds insulting. It's much more tactful to put it after a positive question. You can make a negative question more palatable by doing some self-disclosure. In other words, you could first ask, "Tell me about a time you had to be flexible in dealing with a customer," and then follow up by saying, "I know I've had many times when I looked back at a negotiation and wished I had stood my ground. Can you tell me about a time you were too flexible and gave in too easily?"

Typically what managers do is conduct an interview that just covers surface, cosmetic issues. They spread it too thin. They ask vague questions like, "Tell me about yourself?" or "Tell me what you did on your last job?" After a few of these vague questions, the time is up. Guess what? They haven't learned anything useful about the candidate. The most useful thing would be to know if the person is any good. They haven't found that out. A better approach is to limit the focus of the interview to a few projects, work assignments, or accomplishments. Then, dig in with very specific questions to find out what this person tried to do on the job, how he tried to do it, what obstacles he tried to overcome, and how things turned out. You need to continue to drill down until you're satisfied that you have an indication of whether you're dealing with a person who has a track record of success, a track record of failure, or a mixed track record.

You don't have to cover everything someone has done because behavior tends to follow a pattern. In other words, once you know how someone handled one difficult situation, you can judge that they'll handle every difficult situation pretty much the same way. A bowler who has a 110 average isn't likely to roll a 300 game. They'll probably continue to roll games around 110. The bowler with the 285 average is much more likely to roll a 300 game. Behaviors (and bowling scores) tend to follow a pattern.

If you're interviewing someone fresh out of school, obviously you'll have a more difficult time looking at evidence of accomplishment. Still, there will be things that the outstanding person has done that should point to likelihood of continued success. They've probably overcome obstacles, done volunteer work, held summer jobs, done special projects for professors, or held leadership positions on campus. The advantage of hiring people with no full-time experience is that they come cheaper. The disadvantage is that they certainly are more of a risk, no matter *how* good you are as an interviewer.

Surround Yourself with the Best

There's nothing more important than surrounding yourself with outstanding people. You owe it to yourself and your organization. Yet, for many managers, it's a bother. They act like it's their lowest priority instead of their highest. The candidates you want are the candidates everyone else wants. You can't always offer them the most money, but you can always treat them better than anyone else. If you've got a 9:00 A.M. appointment with the candidate, show up at 9:00 A.M. sharp, not 9:15. If you tell them that someone else will interview them at 10:00 A.M., make sure that someone else is there. If you tell them you'll get back to them by Friday, get back to them by Friday. There's no excuse for not doing these things. If you're dying, delegate the responsibility to someone when you're still on your deathbed. No excuses. Candidates are watching carefully. Everything you say you're going to do has to get done. If you break commitments during the interview process, people will assume that you'll break commitments on the job. In other words, you can't be trusted.

Try not to ever lose an outstanding candidate. Don't procrastinate. Don't give them the foolish "We're going through the first round of screening and we'll get back to you when we're ready" routine. Jump on them the way one of your salespeople would jump on a purchase order. Don't be afraid to tell them how good they are. Obviously, don't commit to something if you don't have the authority to carry out the commitment. Don't tell the job candidate, "I expect we'll be making you an offer," because you can get into trouble if that person goes back and resigns. Lawyers don't like that kind of thing. But, when you think the job candidates are good, tell them. It's like dating. If you're afraid to tell someone how you feel about them, you have no one to blame but yourself if they go off and marry someone else. At the very least, tell them how impressed you are with their accomplishments.

If you have to have job candidates interview with someone else, set up the appointment on the spot and tell them you'll get back to them to confirm it. That also gives you a chance to "keep them warm." The more times you e-mail or phone them, the better. Just like the way your salespeople deal with prospects. Ask them what other offers they have and get the details about base salary, stock options, bonus arrangement, or other benefits. I don't think I've ever had an applicant who wouldn't give me that information. Ask them straight out, "If we made you an offer, would you accept?" or "Are we your top choice?" or "What concerns do you have about the job?" You might want to have a vice president call the person to indicate how impressed she is with the resume and what good things she has heard about the applicant. Most important, turn things around quickly. If you've got a slow-moving bureaucracy, streamline it. Good people don't last long on the job market. You can't always offer the most money, but you can move faster than anyone else. If the candidate already has other offers, don't neglect to ask her to get back to those companies and ask for more time to make a decision. What do you have to lose? Why *not* ask the candidate to do that? You can be very direct and say, "Would you do me a favor and not accept another offer until we're able to get back to you?" All is fair in love, war, and recruiting.

Sell the Job

A lot of managers think they don't have to sell a candidate. They think their company sells itself, or it's the job of the human resources department to sell the candidate. Nothing could be further from the truth. You can't always offer the most money, but you can sell the job the best.

By "selling," I don't mean misrepresenting. Always be truthful with an applicant. Never exaggerate or withhold information. It doesn't do you, or anyone else, any good for a candidate to say a few weeks or months into the job, "This isn't what I thought it would be." By "selling," I mean putting a positive spin on things. Knowing how to describe the job in an enticing way. Talking about "opportunities" and not "problems." I also don't recommend putting anyone on the interview schedule who doesn't speak of the job and the company in positive terms. Even if you have the best technical gurus, if they can't represent the company well, you don't want them to be interviewing potential job candidates. You must be able to give a candidate a satisfactory answer to the question, "Why should I come to work for you?" Here are some good ways to sell a job:

• *Use self-disclosure.* This is one instance where talking about yourself is a good thing to do. Talk about why you joined the company, the things you've been able to do there, and what excites you about the job opportunity you are trying to fill. If you can, say something like, "I never thought I'd get the chance to . . . ."

• *Give specifics.* Just like you don't want vague, theoretical answers to your questions, so, too, you shouldn't give vague, theoretical descriptions of the job opportunity. For example, if an interviewer said, "There's a lot of room for growth here," it wouldn't impress me. Everyone says that. On the other hand, if the interviewer said, "We've promoted 276 people so far this year," that information would definitely impress me. It sounds real. I believe it.

• *Be a good storyteller.* Talk about specific people and the things they've been able to do at your company. Every organization has had its share of heroes. Know their stories and tell them. They don't have to be members of management, just anyone who has done extraordinary things. If you don't know these stories, do some research.

• *Describe what holders of this particular job have been able to do.* If someone who once held this position is now a vice president, that's a great incentive. Maybe someone in this position won some sort of company award or received a patent or published a paper. Find out real examples of what people have been able to do or how far they've gone.

• *Actually listen to the applicant.* As hard as it is to do, paying attention to other people has its advantages. Ask, "What brings you to the job market?" or "What do you enjoy most about your current job?" or "What career plans have you formulated?" Then take notes or memorize answers. As you describe the job, use the applicant's terminology and phraseology.

Start sentences with comments such as, "I know you're interested in . . ." and "As you mentioned . . ." and "You indicated that . . . ." Since people aren't used to being listened to, the impact will be significant. Listening is a key skill that salespeople use to build rapport with customers and prospects. We're not talking about pretending to listen; we're talking about being able to quote them. You really have to listen to be able to do that.

• *Talk about successes.* Find out what awards your company and the people in it have won. Describe the "firsts" and the "onlys." Saying that you've got the lowest employee turnover in your industry, for example, is very impressive. People like to be associated with winners. They love to go home and tell a spouse, "You won't believe this but I interviewed with a company that was named the best . . ." or "This company was the first to . . . ."

• *Treat applicants the way you would customers.* Whether they get a job offer or not, all applicants should go away raving about how professionally they have been treated. They'll tell friends, relatives, neighbors, and others in their professional community. An outstanding reputation is built one transaction at a time, just like you build a customer base. For you to get the cream of the crop, the applicants that everyone else wants, you need the best reputation. Then the best will beat a path to your door. The alternative is to have to run big full-page ads in the newspaper, post your jobs on every website, and pay outlandish employment agency fees. Because your reputation is not good, you'll wind up getting the "bottom of the barrel" applicants—the leftovers that no one else wants.

• *Use your top management.* If you tell them you've got a terrific applicant who needs to be sold, my guess is that they'll be delighted to help you. They're used to selling to customers and most of them will do a good job with applicants. Obviously, don't ask a member of top management who wouldn't dazzle an applicant.

If you have a lot of openings in a job category or if you have a single job that is going to be particularly hard to fill, consider creating a DVD to help you promote the job. You can also use employee orientation material, trade show material, or advertising material from your marketing people. Distribute whatever you come up with the same way AOL used to give out

CDs to every store in town. If you are trying to fill a position in the IT department, then once you've created your "IT pitch," for example, you can use it for all IT openings for years to come. You can also make an impact by filming interviews with current employees in that job category who can talk about how terrific the job is and the thrill they get coming to work each day. Even if they don't talk that way on a normal day, they will in front of a camera. Don't give them a script, though, but have them talk about the job in their own terms.

Use both your human resources department and employment agencies as an extension of your own department. Bring them into your group and educate them about the work being done in your area. Get them excited about the opportunities you have available. If you have a number of openings, invite every contingency agency from your geographic area, as well as the area of specialty. Put on a show for them. The same kind of show you'd put on at a convention or trade show. Make sure there are giveaways for them to take home. Let them know you want their best applicants and that you expect them only to refer people that they have personally interviewed.

Use Creative Sourcing Techniques

Many managers complain that their human resources department doesn't provide candidates in a timely manner. That's like blaming your accounting department because you didn't negotiate a large enough budget for the coming year. More assertive managers regard HR as simply one of the sources of applicants. Figure 5-1 lists a few creative ideas you might try instead of the traditional approaches to finding job candidates.

Promote from Within

Before you consider going to the outside to fill a job opening, make sure you've given everyone internally serious consideration. A sound organizational strategy is to bring people in at entry-level positions and then promote from within. When you hire from the outside, it sends a strong message to people—we don't think any of you are good enough. Everything I've talked about in this chapter applies to both external as well as internal interviewing.

I remember a project that a tough, demanding division manager gave

Figure 5-1. Creative sourcing techniques.

Traditional Approach	More Creative Approach
Use human resources as your sole source of applicants.	Use everyone in your company as a possible source of applicants. Constantly remind them in writing of job openings and make sure there's an enticing employee referral bonus.
Let employees go off to conventions, technical symposiums, and trade shows. Expect that somehow they'll know what your current job openings are.	Give anyone who goes off-site to any sort of gathering the list of openings and remind them of the referral bonus. Set the expectation that they're always going for two purposes, and one of them is to recruit candidates. When they return, ask them how many people they referred.
Get lists of laid-off employees from other companies and contact those employees.	Have someone contact the people who have not been laid off and see if they "know anyone" who'd be interested in interviewing with you. These people are likely upset with all the upheaval in their present company and might be very willing to interview.
Hope a good person comes your way.	Have your public relations agency or a clipping service look at the press releases or the websites of competitors to identify people who have been recognized for their achievements. Contact those people directly. Good people tend to be in the news for patents, published papers, or winning various types of awards.
Announce that you'll be interviewing on a college campus and see who signs up.	Have alumni contact department heads, placement offices, and their old professors to find out who the top graduates are. Let them know you've heard good things about them and you'd like to interview with them when you come on campus.
List your job opening with a contingency employment agency or an executive search firm and hope they give your opening some attention.	Hire an experienced contract recruiter. Give them a list of openings and targeted companies and set them up with a telephone and a computer. They'll know what to do after that.

Encounter someone in a bank, retail store, or working in a local business and say, "That's the kind of person we should have in our company."

When you (or anyone else in your company) encounters someone impressive, give them a business card that tells them you're impressed with them and refers them to a company "hotline" or website for information on job openings.

Only look for permanent employees.

Have a staff of temporary employees, co-ops, and interns for peak workload or vacation periods. If they turn out to be particularly good, make them permanent job offers.

Advertise in newspapers or list openings on generic websites.

For each job opening, find out from incumbents what websites or blogs they frequently visit. Advertise on those targeted sites.

Interview when there is an approved requisition. Take months to fill openings.

Interview year-round so that when there is an approved requisition, you already have a number of good candidates lined up.

Only invite current employees and their families to open houses.

Invite members of the geographic as well as technical community to open houses. Put the same type of effort into this event that you would with a trade show. Advertise giveaways, prizes, and special drawings. Have recruiters available for on-the-spot interviews.

List openings with local high schools and colleges.

Establish close relationships with local high schools and colleges. Give projects to their students, have company employees speak to them about career opportunities, and sponsor special events at schools year-round. Be the local employer of choice.

Give lots of money to newspapers, employment agencies, and Internet job listing companies.

Give lots of money to your own employees along with special bonuses. For example, lease a Mercedes or other attractive company car. The person who refers the most people that month gets to drive the Mercedes next month. You can also rent chauffeur-driven limos, offer house-cleaning services, or give away big-screen plasma televisions. Have an employee committee decide what awards would be most enticing. Be sure these incentive programs are reported by local newspapers and television stations. It's more free publicity for your company.

me. I was new to his organization and he asked me for a listing of all the times we had gone outside the company to fill a position in the last five years. And he wanted to know why we had to go to the outside. I presented him with the long list and he asked me what job was first. I breathed a sigh of relief because it was an entry-level accounting job requiring a B.S. in accounting or finance. He said, "Bullfeathers." (Actually, what he said wasn't that, but it was pretty close to it.) Then he said in a booming voice, "Do you want to go out on the manufacturing floor with me and look for people who would love to get into accounting? No one's willing to give them a chance. Do you know what those accounting people do? I'll find 200 people in this building alone who could do that job in their sleep. Someone gave you and me a break in our career. Don't those people deserve it?" I felt guilty, even though I had just arrived and had nothing to do with filling those openings. Then he looked me straight in the eye and said, "Do you want to continue with that list?" I responded with, "That's not necessary. I get the point." I'll never forget what that wise man taught me.

If there's anyone at all who could do the job, you have to fill it from within. Automatically thinking that the best people are outside the organization is a form of prejudice. As is thinking that if someone works for a competitor, they must be good. I certainly don't want the competition's worst people and I'll bet you don't, either. Another common bias is that good people work at good companies and bad people work at bad companies. Not necessarily true. You aren't hiring the company; you're hiring the person. There are plenty of good people who work at bad companies and bad people who work at good companies. Many outstanding people have been fired or laid off. Many poor performers have a string of promotions because they happen to know the right people. Look at every case on its own merits.

Get the New Employee Off to a Good Start

Once new employees come aboard, it's critical that they be made to feel welcome. Be sure someone is there to meet them when they come in and introduce them to others. There's nothing worse than new employees who are treated poorly by "rent-a-cop" security guards packing pistols and attitudes of superiority. New employees don't have badges yet. They're not sure of their new department name. They were told to be there at 8 A.M. and the rent-a-cop tells them their managers don't come in before 9 A.M. They feel like turning around and going home. Make sure the person gets off to a good start. Inform other people in the department whenever new employees are starting so that they don't get greeted with the same questions over and over again: "Who are you?" or "What did you say you'd be doing?" A nice touch is to have announcements with people's backgrounds and personal information about them distributed and posted on bulletin boards ahead of time. If possible, schedule formal orientations for the first week and assign mentors to meet new people at 8 A.M. on their first day, chaperone them around, and take them to lunch.

Some organizations do a better job than others at "onboarding" their new employees. At Walt Disney World, all new cast members (they're not called employees but cast members because they're part of the show) are given a five-day orientation program. Even if someone is a six-week summer employee, they still go through five paid days of "Disney Traditions." Talk about a commitment! My favorite day is Tuesday, when new cast members line up at the end of Main Street, USA before the park opens and face their customers (who are called Guests, with a capital "G," mind you, like God). Asked what Guests look like, the new cast member says, "Nothing special. Ordinary people. Parents yelling at their kids. People on crutches and in wheelchairs. Some old and sick. Nothing special." Then they drop the ropes and these people run to be the first in line for the attractions. Families are united. The old and sick are running. It's a surefire Fountain of Youth. Disney becomes the "Happiest Place on Earth." And these minimum-wage workers who aren't supposed to have much of a work ethic think, "I've got to have the most important job in the world! What a privilege it is to work here!" Then they go out and face the 95-degree temperatures and 95 percent humidity. They don't mind it at all.

So, what do you do in your organization for an orientation program? It's all too common for new employees to be greeted this way: "Oh, hello there. What was your name again? The other people will show you what to do."

I remember a job I started once where my manager was totally unprepared for me. There was no office, no phone, and no computer. I was given a stack of policy manuals and told that I should get familiar with them. That was supposed to be my job for the entire first week. I was feeling pretty discouraged until I overheard the president of the company talking to an administrative assistant about me. I thought I was getting in trouble for using someone else's office while they were traveling that week. Instead, the president came over and welcomed me. He knew who I was and knew my background. I was so impressed. That single act made me feel welcomed. That was almost twenty-five years ago. I remember it to this day. Yes, first impressions are lasting.

Retaining Top Talent

Employees join companies but they leave managers. I've conducted hundreds of new employee orientation sessions. They are a joy. The newcomers are enthusiastic and have the most positive attitudes you can imagine. They're thrilled about joining such a fine company. I've also conducted hundreds of exit interviews. They are a horror show. Many people on their way out are disillusioned and have the most negative attitudes you can imagine about their manager. The departing employee often says, "Look, I'm saying to everyone that there's another opportunity that's too good to turn down, but the truth is I can't wait to get away from my current manager. That person has made my life miserable. Just don't repeat that to anyone."

I've seen some groups with yearly turnover exceeding 100 percent, and when I ask the managers what the problem is, they usually respond by saying, "That's just the way it is in our industry. Nothing we can do about it." I would suggest to you that if you were losing 100 percent of your customers each year, there would be an investigation. Someone would get in trouble. In just about every company I know, the human resources people tell me that someday their top management will want to know why so many people leave. Unfortunately, that day never seems to come.

Employee turnover costs money. Lots of it. Concern costs nothing. Obviously, you can't completely eliminate turnover. But if you can cut it down by, say, 10 percent, it would have a dramatic effect on profitability. The key is taking a proactive approach and preventing potential problems. In other words, rather than training people to deal with customers who are angry about late shipments, a better approach is preventing shipments from being late in the first place. If turnover is the issue, managers need to be alert to signals that an employee is demotivated. Instead of ignoring or discounting these signals, a manager should act immediately to prevent the employee's concerns from growing into thoughts of defection. Signals to watch for would be a sudden drop in productivity, increased absenteeism, not volunteering for projects or assignments, identifying with or referring to departed employees, withdrawal from the group, being more easily irritated by little things, and talking about burnout.

The interview process can do a lot for someone's ego. If employees are being ignored or taken for granted by their current manager, they'll turn somewhere else, and a company interviewing people will roll out the red carpet for them. The hiring manager tells the employee that his background is impressive. The employee talks about being underutilized, and the hiring manager says, "We'd never do that to you. Someone like you could go a long way in our company." It's enticing. The idea is to never put one of your employees in a position where they would want to interview with another company. Once they do, they're halfway out the door.

When you detect signs that your employees are becoming discouraged, meet with them. Tell them how valuable they are and how much they mean to you and the department. Talk about the signs you've noticed and ask if it's an indicator of their being discouraged. Whatever the employees say, you should listen attentively and try and turn it into actions that you or the employees can take. Always thank them for their honesty and reinforce how important they are to you and the department. Don't just drop the subject. Schedule follow-up meetings. If they deny they're discouraged, that's fine. A little bit of attention can go a long way. At least they know you're interested in them.

What to Do When a Top Performer Resigns

If your preventive measures don't work and people give their resignation, all is not lost. Meet with them immediately. The longer you wait, the more likely you are to really lose them. Assuming you don't want them to go, say something like, "I'm shocked to hear you're considering leaving us after just two years. You're a terrific performer and a key part of our organization. I'd like to ask what prompted you to consider looking elsewhere. If you wouldn't mind, I'd like to know the specifics of your proposed new position. I want to try to do whatever I can to have you stay with us." Don't let them go without a fight.

Hopefully, they'll be open with you and you'll take notes so that you can capture their exact words. Typically, you won't be able to respond to their concerns without talking to your manager. So, let them know you'll get back to them quickly. In the meantime, ask them not to tell anyone that they have accepted another offer. The more people they tell, the harder it will be to have them change their mind. Keep saying things like, "Losing a top performer like you would hurt me, the department, and the company. I want to try to provide the same opportunities you're hoping to find at the other company." Even if you're not successful, word will get out that you handled the matter professionally and with a real concern for the employee.

Don't counteroffer with more money. Employees who accept counteroffers are usually gone shortly thereafter because the reasons they decided to look for another job in the first place don't change. The money just delays the inevitable. Besides, once you extend a raise to one employee, you'll have a line of people at your door claiming offers from other companies and threatening to resign if you don't pay them more. They'll figure it's the easiest way to get a raise. That's the wrong message to send. People can always go out and get more money. Dissatisfaction typically stems from problems with the manager. That doesn't mean you can pay people in a below-average manner. Pay people well. If certain people are legitimately underpaid, the time to give them equity adjustments is before the fact, not when they have resigned.

A strategy of simply counteroffering with money can backfire. It can cause the employee to conclude: "They just don't get it. Why are they trying to throw money at me now? If I'm that good, they should have offered me that money before. They always cry broke, but all of a sudden they can find thousands of dollars in the budget to try to convince me to stay. It's insulting. No thanks!"

The worst crime you can commit in an organization is to lose an outstanding person. When that happens, there should be a congressional investigation. What went wrong? How could the situation have been prevented? If you worked for me, I'd say, "Make sure it never happens again." And I don't just mean losing people physically, by having them leave the company. You can also lose your employees mentally, by having them withdraw their energy and enthusiasm. In some ways, it's better to lose someone physically. At least you get the chance to replace the worker, hopefully with an outstanding performer. When you lose employees mentally, they may be gone forever.

Characteristics of Outstanding Performers

Outstanding people are strong in at least one of three possible areas. The very best, the cream of the crop, are strong in all three areas:

1. *Motivation*. They work harder than anyone else.
2. *Aptitude*. The work just comes easy to them.
3. *Experience*. They've been in the right places and done the right thing.

Outstanding people can and should be found at every level of the organization. I remember being named HR director for a company. In that capacity I went to the different manufacturing facilities meeting people. The third plant I visited was amazing. They called it the "flagship" plant. It was a showpiece. It was set up for plant tours. There were roped-off areas with process flow diagrams. You could live next door to one of the other plants around the world but the company would fly you to this plant for a tour. The Occupational Safety and Health Administration (OSHA) was in all the time, but not to catch anyone doing anything wrong. OSHA actually used the plant as a model of good manufacturing practices.

You could feel the energy and enthusiasm the moment you walked into the building. If you dropped a piece of paper, ten people would dive to pick it up. There were signs and banners all over the place. Not the generic type that management buys through mail order, but real signs written by hand by real people. I was just blown away. I said, "Whose responsible for all this?" They said, "George is the key guy." I responded, "He must be a great plant manager." They laughed and said, "He's not the plant manager." So I said, "He must be some department head, then." They said, "You've got it all wrong. George works in maintenance." I thought he must be at least a lead or section head. They told me that there was an hourly classification system that started with H-1. George was the only H-1 they had. He was the janitor.

Needless to say, I sought out George. He was amazing. George would go over to someone and say, "How's your presentation coming? Will you be ready by Friday? If you'd like, I'd be happy to stay and rehearse with you tonight." He'd go over to the next person and say, "Remember on your next report to take into account the variable that . . . ." When someone was out sick, he'd welcome them back with a "How are you? We really missed you yesterday. It's good to have you back." George told me about how he created contests, banners, and slogans because, he said, "People get lazy and sloppy. You've got to keep them from getting in a rut. The place depends on me." When someone feels that way, they are almost always a top performer. I asked him why he wasn't a higher grade than an H-1. He said, "They're after me all the time to bid on a higher-level job. I don't have any interest. I love what I do. I have free reign. I make my own schedule. No one is looking over my shoulder. It's the perfect job. An H-2 would be confined to a particular workstation. I don't have any interest." When someone says, "I love what I do," that's another sure sign of a top performer.

George retired at age 78. His retirement party attracted 3,500 people. It was the biggest retirement party I've ever been to. He was introduced to a thunderous standing ovation. It was a bigger ovation than I've ever heard for any president or vice president I've ever known. As I think back, George probably had more of an impact on that business than any company president or vice president I've ever known. Outstanding people are like that. You want to hire as many people like George as you can. Not just at the top, but at every level. A great building is built from the ground up. It starts with a strong foundation. Without one, the building will crumble one day.

When you're fortunate enough to have outstanding people working for you, you can't treat them like everyone else. I know managers who say, "I can't play favorites. The other people will be jealous." That's baloney. A member of the Chicago Bulls once told me about an incident with a brash rookie. It was an extremely close game. The score was tied, in fact, with just seconds to go. Doug Collins was coach at the time. He called a time-out and drew up a play for Michael Jordan to take the last shot, as was the custom. The rookie complained, "Michael always gets to take the last shot. Why not fake it to Michael and I'll take the shot." Doug responded angrily, "When you become Michael Jordan, I'll let you take the shot. Until then, watch and learn." Of course, Jordan hit the winning shot. He always hit the winning shot. That's what outstanding people do. They always come through. Treat them like everybody else and they'll start to behave like everybody else. You'll always have brash rookies around. Give them the incentive to become as good as the outstanding person. Then, their time will come.

If you don't take care of your special, gifted people, some other company will. Your best performers will think, "I don't get it. I'm doing top-flight work and what do I get for it? Nothing. The boss doesn't seem to care. I'm beginning to think management wants mediocrity."

Top performers have three characteristics that are always present:

1. *They have an outstanding reputation.* People come to them for help and advice—both from inside and outside their organization. They've gotten the highest allowable merit increases and bonuses, the biggest stock option grants, and the outstanding performance review ratings.

2. *They produce extraordinary results.* They perform miracles on a regular basis. They somehow find a way to do things they shouldn't be able to do. Ask them about it and they'll give a long history (often beginning with their childhood) of accomplishing things that others thought impossible.

3. *They constantly strive to make improvements.* They're not satisfied with things being "all right" or "good enough." They want to make them better. Because of this characteristic, poor managers may regard them as complainers and malcontents. Look at the most successful entrepreneurs. They all have this drive for improvement.

I would look to hire people who have the aforementioned characteristics, encourage all employees to be like that, and reward them if they exhibit any of those behaviors.

Extraordinary Managers—People with a Cause

So many people spend their time working *in* the business that they don't work *on* the business. They're involved so closely in the day-to-day workings that they don't take a step back and think about why they do what they do and the impact they have on their work teams. Extraordinary managers point the way. One of the things I like to do in the classroom is have everyone quickly point north. Invariably, everyone will point in different directions. That doesn't mean that the people are bad; it just means they need direction. A leader must say, "This will be our north!" in a convincing fashion. Will the leader be right? Not necessarily. But, without someone taking charge and making the call, people will just argue among themselves or go in opposite directions. A leader always has the right to change direction. I would have no problem with a leader who says, "I just got new information. We need to change our direction." At least the leader is taking a position. The worst managers say, "I need to wait and see. I'll let you know when 'they' have decided." Of course, the worst manager never gets back to anyone.

To be an outstanding manager, you need a compelling cause. You have to stand for something. Something you can get excited about and, in turn, get others excited about, too. What would your people say *your* cause is? Some of the best leaders I've known have worked in areas that would seem pretty mundane—payroll, accounts payable, purchasing, and tax accounting. What differentiates them from ordinary managers is that they stand for something special. They want something special for their department. Their cause excites people and attracts the best in their field. You don't want to be "easy" on people. That puts them to sleep. Makes them "brain dead." It's like having a twelve-year-old Little Leaguer only hit off of a tee. That's fine for a five- or six-year-old just learning how to swing a bat, but a twelve-year-old needs a bigger challenge. On the other hand, you don't want to ask people to do the ridiculous. Don't have the twelve-year-old Little Leaguer play on the high school team. It will destroy his self-confidence. He'll begin to believe he isn't any good. He'll probably quit the game. I like to illustrate this concept with the "Wow!" graph (see Figure 6-1). The "Wow!" point is different for everyone.

Napoleon said it well when he said, "Leaders give people hope!" The

Figure 6-1. The "Wow!" point.

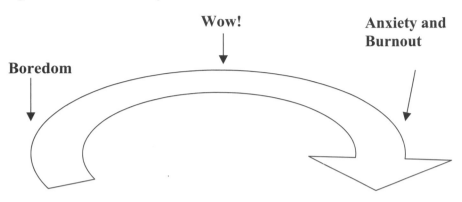

interesting thing is that you don't actually have to reach your lofty goal. It's the journey that's important. For instance, your goal could be to win an Olympic gold medal. Even if you finish last, that's pretty darn good. You were one of the best in the world. You were in the big race. You can tell your grandchildren that you were in the big race. How many people can say that? No one remembers Alexander the Mediocre. We only remember Alexander the Great. Shoot for something that no one has ever done before, or do something better than anyone has done before. If you want to be remembered, you have to aim high.

Your cause could be something that seems insignificant to others. To you, it means everything. For example, I started a campaign to improve our employment offer-to-acceptance ratio. We would get an acceptance about 21 percent of the time when we made a job offer. Are there other things that are important to a human resources function? Of course. But I cared about our getting the applicants we wanted. So I made it my cause. I had the human resources people visit companies where the offer-to-acceptance ratio was as high as 50 percent. I had them talk to applicants who had turned us down over the past five years to find out exactly why they turned us down. We brainstormed ideas as to what we could do to raise that key ratio. We trained our managers in how to maintain applicant self-esteem in an interview. We did all the things I discussed in Chapter 5, on interviewing. One time we even got the president of the company to pull someone out of a meeting to ensure that an applicant wouldn't be left waiting. Interestingly enough, the president only had to do it once. No manager was late to an interview after that.

Our offer-to-acceptance ratio soared to 94 percent. It's the highest I've ever heard of. Newspapers and magazines wrote about us. Employment agencies and college placement offices told people that no one ever turned us down. It evolved into a mystique. Because of it, we were able to attract the best people, the ones that everyone else wants.

Pick a cause. Something that you can get passionate about and something your top management will support. Do it today! Your cause has to be something that your people will believe will benefit the organization. They have to believe they are real participants in something seen as important and worth working toward. You must demonstrate your personal commitment through specific actions. Your words aren't enough. It's deeds that count. If you sacrifice for the cause, others will take notice and be more likely to follow your lead. Make sure you keep top management informed and visible in supporting your efforts. People are always keeping an eye on what top management is supporting and participating in.

Gaining Alignment

Your department is like a rowboat and your team members are like the rowers. You want them pulling in the same direction. It's your job to set that direction. You may say, "Things are unsettled now. I need to wait before I set the direction." Bad choice. It's better to set the direction now, based on what you know. You can always change the direction. Without direction, the rowers will all go their own way and fight against each other. They'll churn up a lot of water, but the boat won't go anywhere. Once in a while, unfortunately, you get someone who won't head in the right direction. You've got to say to that person, "We're going this way. If you don't want to come, you have to get off the boat."

What are the differences between those who are aligned on a cause, a vision, a mission, or whatever you want to call it, and those who are not? Here are some:

Those Who Aren't Aligned	Those Who Are Aligned
Work for money only	Work for a cause
Find satisfaction outside of work	Find satisfaction in the work itself

Those Who Aren't Aligned	Those Who Are Aligned
Just put in their time	Feel it's important to put in their time and energy
Aren't sure of how their efforts contribute to the organization	Know how their efforts contribute to the organization
Describe work in terms of activity	Describe work in terms of outcomes

Make sure you give your people specific goals that will result in the achievement of your cause. One thing I've always done is grade people on "A" goals—that is, those goals that would result directly in achievement of the cause. The "B" goals would be important, too, but more related to the routine day-to-day business. The "C" goals would be those that are worth working on only if time allows. We would generate point values, such as five points for attainment of an "A" goal, three points for a "B" goal, and one point for a "C" goal. There would be a department score each week as well as individual scores. When you make these scores visible, I can almost guarantee you that the results will improve week by week. It becomes like a contest. People are naturally competitive. It's one of the many things that makes work more than "work."

In addition to your employees, there are many others who can help or hinder you in your cause. These people include your manager, the person your manager works for, your peers, and employees in other departments. These people could provide ideas, information, resources, and other forms of support. You've got to build alliances with them. Go to their staff meetings. Visit them on the job. Have you and your staff constantly evangelize ideas. People forget. They lose focus. They need constant reminders.

On the other hand, there are always people who will see your ideas as threatening the status quo. They're jealous. They're afraid. Sometimes, that person may resist what you want to do because a friend of theirs is resistant to your ideas. You need a plan to deal with those who are likely to oppose your cause. Don't ignore them. Try to include them in planning. Invite them to your staff meetings. I once did a research project on yielding or conforming to groups. We put people in a darkened room and asked them how much a pinpoint of light appeared to move. The actual movement was about one-sixteenth of an inch. Unknown to the subjects, we had some people who were part of the experiment "planted" inside the group to make outrageous claims about the pinpoint of light wavering two or three inches. As long as we had these people in the group, we could get the other people to see things that weren't there.

If you put a subject in a group where everyone else is part of the experiment, you could get the subject to say things he knows aren't true. For example, if a group of people is asked, "Who was the first president of the United States?" and they answer "Thomas Jefferson," there would be a high likelihood that the subject would also answer with "Thomas Jefferson." In the debrief, the subject would say, "I knew it was George Washington, but I didn't want to look stupid in front of the group. So I went along with everyone else." Kind of like the lynch mobs in the Old West. Or what kids do in a gang. So, as a leader, you can talk to someone one-on-one to convince that person of something. If you're smarter, you'll bring others along with you or have that person come to one of your meetings. There's a significantly greater likelihood the person will want to go along with the group.

To facilitate the attainment of your cause, vision, or mission, you should also consider questions such as, "How should the structure of my organization change?" or "What policies and procedures need to change?" or "What new knowledge or skills will my people need?" The time to initiate such changes is before they're needed. It's much better than trying to fix things that are already broken. So, as you pitch your cause to those around you, solicit ideas for what needs to be done differently.

Outstanding managers have a positive and hopeful vision of the future. They show how mutual interests can be met through commitment to a common purpose. When I say commitment, I mean it in the strongest possible sense. Someone with true commitment will sacrifice anything for the cause. They're willing to give their all, like a soldier in combat, for the cause.

Action Items for Developing Your Ability to Attract and Retain Top Talent

Attracting/Retaining Top Talent—Creating a work environment that attracts and retains the best employees with the motivation, aptitude, and experience you want.

• Craft a vision statement for your functional area. Be sure it has the buy-in of your management and your employees. Then "take it on the road" to staff meetings of other departments, community organizations, and local schools and colleges. Typically, the shorter and more dramatic your message, the better. Think of how much mileage Nike has gotten out of just three words: "Just Do It." Make your message as omnipresent as Nike's.

• Periodically meet with your people to revisit how close or far away you are from making that vision a reality. Each time, do an assessment of past actions and brainstorm ideas for new actions.

• Be sure to "walk the talk." Remember that talk is cheap and intentions are irrelevant. It's actions that count. Plan daily, weekly, monthly, and quarterly actions and then gauge their effectiveness. Remember, the key factor is your enthusiasm and commitment.

• Involve your key people first. Tell the opinion leaders and those that are the experienced technical people that the others look up to them and you'll be relying on them for help. Be sure they're on your side and will back you up. If not, you may have to ask them to either give you their full commitment or to move on.

• Think of how you should market your message. Why should your customer buy in? What's in it for them? Can you build brand awareness for your inspiring vision of the future? What marketing collateral will you need? It takes more than hats and T-shirts, but they're a start.

• Publicly reward those employees whose actions support your vision and strategic goals. Make them into heroes. On the other hand, if someone has voiced opposition or isn't willing to give you a full commitment, make your expectations clear in writing and don't delay in taking appropriate disciplinary action.

• Look at your entire organization structure and the way work and tasks are organized. If there's a better way, the sooner you improve the structure the better. Be sure new roles are clearly defined.

• Analyze who has succeeded and who hasn't in your area of responsibility. Look for trends. Don't repeat the hiring mistakes made in the past. Also, be sure to understand the hiring successes of the past so that you can repeat them.

• Get your people together to generate ideas on who should be hired and how those people should be recruited. Give everyone the responsibility of ensuring your group is stocked with the best possible talent.

• Similarly, ask your people about your group's orientation process and how it can be improved. You want new people to be "ramped up" in record time. Don't allow someone to be assimilated on a hit-or-miss basis.

• Identify peers who have stocked their organization with top talent. Find out how they've done it.

• Keep a year-round eye out for talent. Even if you have no current openings, it's helpful to know who might be a job candidate should a need arise. If you come across someone outstanding, consider hiring in advance of a need, because it might give you some bench strength. So many departments find themselves in dire straits: "We're swamped. We've got six open requisitions, two people on maternity leave, three on vacation, two out sick. . . ." Try to get ahead of the game. You might consider bringing on temporaries or interns. You might even want to become part of a job rotation program, so you can "try before you buy."

• Do long-term organizational planning. Cut a requisition well in advance so you'll have plenty of time to search out the best candidate. Recognize that a job you plan to add to your organization four or five years from now could be an internal promotion if you begin preparing someone for it now.

Planning and Organizing
Your Group's Performance

Building Capability and Accountability

I've always been interested in top performers and why they're so good. I was named a human resources director for a company and was visiting manufacturing facilities for the first time. I was out in Missouri and asked the local HR manager who the best operator was out on the manufacturing floor. She started to point someone out to me, but then there was a telephone call for her, so she excused herself to take the call. I went over to the person and congratulated him on being a top performer. He responded the way many top performers do. He said, "Oh, really. News to me. No one tells you anything around this damn place." I continued to ask him questions. He swelled with pride as he described how he did his job. I told him to keep up the good work. The HR manager came back and asked me if I talked to Tom. I said, "Who's Tom? I talked to Fred." She said, "Oh, no. You talked to the wrong guy. Fred is the worst we've got. He's so bad we're probably going to have to fire him." Needless to say, I couldn't wait to get out of Missouri.

Three weeks later, the HR manager gave me a call. She said that Fred had gone from worst to first. "What did you say to him? How did you do that?" I told her it was a mistake. Then I began to think. I congratulated him on being so good. Could I have been the first person to ever treat him well? I remembered what he said to me: "News to me. No one tells you anything around here." Is it that simple? Do people respond according to the way you treat them? If so, I stumbled upon some magic principle. So, I started to do some research. I'll share a little of that with you.

The Self-Fulfilling Prophecy

Is it really magic? Well, it seems that way. The term "self-fulfilling prophecy" was first used by Robert Merton and was dealt with extensively in *Social Theory and Social Structure* (1968). Magic was certainly involved in the ancient myth that Ovid told in the tenth book of *Metamorphoses*. According to the story, the sculptor Pygmalion sought to create an ivory statue of the ideal woman. The result, which he named Galatea, was so beautiful that Pygmalion fell desperately in love with his own creation. He prayed to the goddess Venus to bring Galatea to life. Venus granted him his wish and the couple lived happily ever after. The other name, therefore, for the self-fulfilling prophecy is "the Pygmalion effect."

The London play *Pygmalion,* brought to Broadway as *My Fair Lady,* is the story of Professor Henry Higgins, who insists that he can take a Cockney flower girl and, with some vigorous training, pass her off as a duchess. He succeeds. But a key point lies in the comment by the flower girl, Eliza Doolittle, who says, " . . . the difference between a lady and a flower girl is not how she behaves, but how she's treated." Once she's treated as a lady, Eliza wants to continue to be treated that way. It's very difficult to be treated poorly once you've been treated well.

So much of being an outstanding manager involves building people's self-image and capability. A simple truth is:

- *Bad managers* lose the confidence of their people.
- *Good managers* inspire people to have confidence in them.
- *Great managers* inspire people to have confidence in themselves.

The concept of the self-fulfilling prophecy can be summarized in four key principles:

1. We form certain expectations of people or events.
2. We communicate those expectations with various cues.
3. People tend to respond to these cues by adjusting their behavior to match them.
4. The result is that the original expectation comes true.

You're not convinced? A whole body of research says you should be. Robert Rosenthal and Lenore Jacobson (1968) worked with elementary schoolchildren from eighteen classrooms. They randomly chose 20 percent of the children from each room and told the teachers they were "intellectual bloomers." They explained that these children could be expected to show remarkable gains during the year. The experimental children showed average IQ gains of two points in verbal ability, seven points in reasoning, and four points in overall IQ. Treat kids like they're smart and they'll become smarter? Of course! It's as simple as those schoolchildren being treated better, paid more attention to, and given more encouragement. They liked being treated that way, worked hard, and were more attentive in class. It had a predictably positive effect on them—they actually *became* intellectual bloomers.

Rosenthal also described an experiment in which he told a group of students in an experimental psychology class that he had developed a strain of superintelligent rats that could run mazes very quickly. He then told half of the students that they had the new "maze bright" rats and the other half that they got "maze dull" rats. Of course, all the rats in both groups were chosen at random. The rats believed to be bright improved daily in running the maze—they ran faster and more accurately. In one measure, for example, the "dull" rats refused to budge from the starting point 29 percent of the time while the "bright" rats refused only 11 percent of the time. Rats react to the way they're treated? You bet! The bright rats were held differently, smiled at, talked to, and encouraged by the students.

The students also wrote performance reviews on their rats. And don't you know which rats were judged to be easier to work with and better behaved? That's right. The "maze bright" ones.

There's a true story about a horse named Clever Hans who, in 1911, was owned by a German mathematician, Wilhelm Von Osten. Hans was sensational. You could ask him what three and two were and he would tap out five with his hoof. No one knew how he did it. In fact, Von Osten swore that even he didn't know how the horse was able to do it. He said he had never trained him to do tricks. Researchers went to study the wonder horse. The first thing they found was that Clever Hans was clever only when people expected him to be. In other words, if you believed the horse could do the tricks, he was able to do them. If you were a skeptic, Hans wasn't clever at all. They also found that Hans had to be able to see the questioner. From this information, they realized that Hans was simply an attentive horse. Someone would lean forward or give some other subtle clue to alert Hans when he should start or stop tapping. The clues were involuntary and as seemingly insignificant as the raising of an eyebrow or the dilation of nostrils. Someone who didn't believe Hans could do the tricks didn't give off the nonvoluntary clues. People (and animals) are constantly picking up the clues that we unknowingly give them.

It's no accident that some managers complain that their people aren't very good and avoid responsibility. When you talk to those people, you realize the managers are right. Yet there are other managers in similar departments who say their people are particularly good and love to take on responsibility. When you talk to those people, you realize those managers are right, too. Could it be the difference is in the managers, not in the people? That's usually the case.

The simple truth is that almost all of us behave according to the way we're treated. If you keep telling a teenager, for example, that she is worthless and isn't going to amount to anything, it's got to have an impact. On the other hand, if you sincerely and repeatedly tell the teenager that she is wonderful and is going to be a big success at anything she attempts, that has to have an impact, too. Virtually all of us have had a manager who believed in us, worked with us, and gave us responsible assignments. We likely responded by doing our best work for that person. In the end, the boss said, "See. I knew it all along." Unfortunately, virtually all of us have had a manager who didn't believe in us, criticized us constantly, and didn't give us anything responsible to do. We likely responded by doing our worst work for that person. In the end, that boss too said, "See. I knew it all along."

Like the teacher with the student, the student with the rat, and the questioner with the horse, managers have a profound impact on the success or failure of employees. Ever wonder why those "high potential" employees do so well when they are brought in? They're often given rotational assignments and special projects. Top management takes a keen interest in these superstars. Guess what? They tend to have very good careers. Were they any better than anyone else? Maybe. Maybe not. It makes you wonder. Is it, "I'll believe it when I see it," or is it really, "I'll see it when I believe it"?

Making People Feel Important

Making people feel important gives you some real payback. A little over a year ago, a young engineering manager told me about a problem he was having with one of his older engineers. He said, "He's got a bad back, so he calls in a lot saying he can't make it in. I try to be nice to him and tell him to take as much time off as he needs. I tell him not to worry about it. We'll cover for him. Take as much time off as you need. But he's out more and more all the time. I don't know what to do." I told the manager he was doing it all wrong. "What do you mean?" he asked. I said that the next time the engineer called in complaining about his back, the manager should say, "We need you. You're critically important to us. We can't do without you. The customer will want you and no one else to do the installation." He tried that. It's been over a year. The engineer hasn't been out since.

So many managers spend their time trying to make themselves feel important that they neglect spending time on making their people feel important. Some managers (always the worst ones) declare proudly, "I just leave my people alone. I keep out of their way." Ignoring someone invariably produces disastrous results. In fact, in ancient societies when someone was declared a "nonperson" for a serious crime and everyone in a village was required to ignore them, they'd typically waste away and die soon thereafter.

I remember one time coming home after a tough day at work. I just wanted to sit on the couch and read the newspaper. My three-year-old jumped up on my lap and wanted to play. I said, "No, Scott. Naughty, Scott. Leave Daddy alone. Maybe I'll play with you later." He began to do what three-year-olds usually do when they're ignored—he threw a truck at the television and banged on the walls with a hammer. My wife saw what was going on and tried to help. She said, "No, Scott. Naughty, Scott. Leave Daddy alone. Unless you stop, I'll take you in your room and give you a time-out." With all the wisdom of a three-year-old, he looked at her and said, "Can Daddy take me in my room and give me a time-out?" Ignoring someone is the worst thing you can do. It's a death sentence. Eventually every top performer will say, "I do heroic work around this place. No one seems to care. I'm beginning to think it's just not worth it."

You don't have to spend a million bucks to make someone feel like a million bucks. People need to know their work is recognized and appreciated. Many managers say, "My people know how I feel about them." But when you ask employees, they have no idea how the manager feels about them. Something gets lost in the translation. When I ask managers how much praise and recognition they give their people on a "1" to "10" scale, with "10" as the highest, the typical response is an "8." When I ask the people who work for them how much praise and recognition they get from their manager, the typical response is a "4." Indeed, something gets lost in the translation. For instance, it's not unusual for a manager to say, "You didn't do a half-bad job on that project," or "That turned out all right. I was really surprised." A lot of times the manager will say, "We have a great relationship. We kid around with each other all the time." The employee's version of events? "That manager is a sarcastic jerk. All he ever does is put me down."

Some managers think a merit increase is a good enough way to show praise and recognition. They're kidding themselves. All employees know, either through official or unofficial channels, what the merit guidelines will be. If they figure they'll be getting about a 4 percent raise and that's what they get, they're satisfied. If they get less than that, they're angry. It's rare that they wind up getting more than they expect. So, for most people, the merit increase is a nonevent. It amounts to a few extra dollars that they've probably already spent. Especially if it's given in the usual cavalier manner in a performance review after the manager humiliates them with a bunch of grade-school talk about "work habits" and "citizenship" and "attitude."

The good news is that you'll always have an unlimited budget for praise and recognition. No one can ever take that away from you. An occasional "thank you" goes a long way. But there's something that's even better than a "thank you." What really has a positive effect is a token of appreciation. Something people can touch, feel, hold in their hand, and show to others.

I remember conducting a program at General Motors. There was a woman in the class who told this story:

"I found out, by accident, that there's something much more powerful than verbal praise. I took over a group of eighteen hard-core union autoworkers. The least senior person had twenty-six years with General Motors. They used to make fun of him all the time and call him 'junior' because his seniority was so light. They used to give him all the worst jobs to do. The group had never worked for a woman before. They totally ignored me. I was so discouraged that I was ready to quit. One day, though, one of the technicians solved a tough engineering problem. It turned out he saved the company about a quarter of a million dollars that day. I went out to thank him, but his shift had already left. What I decided to do was write a note in the log that a technician from one shift passes over to the technician on the next shift. I wrote, 'I really want to thank you for the over-and-above work you did today. You saved us a quarter of a million dollars in production and I really appreciate it.' The next day the technician came in and opened his log. He couldn't believe it! Evidently he had never seen pure, unadulterated praise from a member of management. He called over all the other technicians. There was a big crowd of people around his workstation, all pointing to the log. I was accepted by the group and, at the start of every shift from that day forward, everyone would run to their log to see if I wrote anything nice to them."

Committing something to writing gives a powerful message! Sending a copy to all the vice presidents and directors you can think of also delivers a powerful message: I'm proud of what this person has done and I want everyone to know it. Are these commonsense principles practiced in the workplace? A recent study conducted by Dr. Gerald Graham found that "personal congratulations by my manager for doing a good job" was ranked first out of sixty-five workplace incentives. Yet, 58 percent of the employees in the study said they seldom, if ever, received a thank you from their manager. Ranked second was a personal note for good performance written by a manager, yet 76 percent of the employees reported seldom, if ever, receiving such a note of thanks.

A manager should be just as alert to what interests a person as a salesman is to what interests a prospect. If someone talks about their golf game all the time, maybe a set of golf balls would be a nice token of appreciation. If they mention they didn't bring an umbrella to work on a rainy day because they lost theirs, a new umbrella would be a nice token of appreciation. If you don't know the person very well, a quick call to a spouse or a significant other might yield some clues as to what would give them a "charge." It's also awfully nice to say to the spouse something like, "Your husband has really done a terrific job on the big project. We'd like to thank him in some small way." That's like getting double mileage.

One of the best employee awards is given out by NASA. It's a statue of Snoopy sitting on his doghouse. The "Silver Snoopy" has virtually no monetary value, but it's the way they give the award that is so significant. They invite someone's family in for the presentation. Imagine if your little son or daughter took a note into class saying, "Junior's mom is being given an award for service to her country. She's an American hero. Please excuse Junior on Tuesday from 11 A.M. to 1 P.M. for the awards luncheon." Do you think the teacher might read the note to the class? Do you think Junior might be proud of Mom? Do you think Junior would remember it for the rest of his life? Wow! What a great incentive. They also put the person's picture, along with a story, into the local newspaper. A genuine astronaut presents the award. Family, friends, and neighbors see the newspaper article. Mom would buy souvenir copies. Total cost of the recognition is next to nothing.

Be careful, though, because what's a reward for one person can be a punishment for someone else. I once worked at a company where we wanted to increase donations to the United Way. The idea was that everyone who gave a "Fair Share" would have their names put in a big drum. A name would be drawn and the winner would get an all-expense-paid trip to the Bahamas for a week. We turned the drum and felt we were really lucky that an hourly worker from the warehouse had his name drawn. Needless to say, we immediately sent out press releases, scheduled cable television coverage, and made speeches. Eventually someone wandered out to the warehouse to find this guy. He said, "I've heard about this Bahamas trip of yours. Sorry, I'm not interested." As you might expect, the company representative said, "You *have* to be interested. You have to go. If we make an exception for you, we'll have to make an exception for everyone. This would establish a dangerous precedent. You're really developing a bad attitude." The warehouse worker explained that he didn't actually enter the contest. He always gave a "Fair Share." He went on to say that his wife just came home from the hospital with twins and they now had five children under five years old. "So you see," he said, "a week's vacation, as nice as it would be, is impractical for us. If you really want to help us out, give us a year's supply of diapers." The company continued to argue with him and he wound up quitting. What's a reward for one person can be a punishment for someone else.

I've known vice presidents who thought that having breakfast with them would be a wonderful reward for the lowly workers. They think, "Just being in my exalted presence will lift their spirits." What happens?

Many of the people chosen at random for the "reward" call in sick the day of the breakfast. Guess what? They're genuinely sick. Just the thought of sharing a meal with a vice president sickens them. As I said, what's a reward for one person can be a punishment for someone else.

The best possible token of appreciation is when someone says to you, "How did you know?" It means you've done a little bit of research. You found out what would be most appropriate for that person. You've done something you didn't have to do and it's something personalized just for them. That's what people like the most. I once worked for a man who really understood this principle. On someone's five- or ten-year service anniversary day, the usual award from the company was something like a gold tie tack. A generic, one-size-fits-all gift that no one really had much use for. The kind of item people usually throw in a drawer. But he gave them a personalized, handwritten note thanking them for their accomplishments. And, by God, he listed those accomplishments. So, low-level hourly workers would get a personalized note from a vice president listing the major projects they worked on and detailing their work history. Wow! People would treasure that note. Many of them would buy the most expensive frame they could find and put it in a prominent place in their home, so they could show it to anyone who visited. Everyone wondered how he did it. It was pretty simple. He just had his administrative assistant keep records on the 3,500 people in the division. But everyone thought he was some kind of genius. Total cost? Again, nothing.

Invariably, when I tell these kinds of stories, managers say, "The problem is that our company's recognition program is inadequate." I stress to them that I'm not talking about the official company recognition program. I'm talking about the kinds of things they, as managers, can and should do on their own. If they don't have official authorization to do it, so much the better. If there's no money in the budget and they have to pay for these things out of their own pocket, so much the better. Typically, it's not the monetary value but the creative thought that has the biggest impact.

The Importance of Coaching

By recognizing accomplishments, outstanding managers encourage people to persist in their efforts. These managers have extremely high expectations of people and teams and let people know that their efforts are appreciated. Any leader in any field of human endeavor says to people, "Come on. You can do it." They believe in people so much that the people begin to believe in themselves. Imagine if a sports coach behaved like too many managers do in a work situation. If a track athlete stumbled and fell, the coach would come over and say, "Look, I told you to run fast. What's wrong with you? Why didn't you listen to me? I'm going to keep my eye on you." But that doesn't happen because both the athlete and the coach know that the coach exists for one reason and one reason only—to help the athlete succeed. The track coach would run to the fallen athlete and say, "Are you all right?" The athlete would probably say, "Coach, I let you down. I lost the race. You worked so hard and believed in me so much. I'm sorry." We all know the coach would say to her, "It's okay. There'll be other races. Let me help you up. We'll start working on the next race right away."

So, ask yourself: What did you do the last time an employee asked you for specific performance feedback? What did you do the last time an employee made a mistake?

Having been a sports writer earlier in my career, I can tell you that outstanding athletes have someone who believes in them. They always talk about Coach So-and-So who wouldn't let them quit. The coach was incredibly patient and yet incredibly demanding at the same time. An interesting combination of characteristics. The coach made them do something 372 times until they got it right. Athletes always say, "I didn't think I could do it, but Coach did. Somehow, Coach knew." I also believe that every outstanding person in a business environment has had a manager or mentor who also believed in them. Who was incredibly patient and yet incredibly demanding at the same time. You can be that person. If you're that person for one other person, you've made a contribution. If you're that person for a number of people, you've done more than your share.

Coaches aren't confused as to whether they're a coach or an athlete. They are mature enough to recognize they have to remain on the sidelines. Imagine a football coach who went on the field of play because it was "crunch time." He might say to the field goal kicker, "This is too important. I'm going to make the field goal." Talk about discouraging someone. The poor player would say, "I get it. Whenever it's important, the coach pushes me off the field and takes over." There are too many "field goal kickers" around organizations who know they're going to get "pushed off the field" because the manager loves to take over difficult situations. That would never happen in the world of sports. The football coach would be fined and maybe suspended for venturing onto the field of play. I propose we fine managers who do work that their people should be doing. Everyone who is promoted to manager should sign a document saying, "It's not about you anymore. The employees are the ones who are going to get the gold medals and get their pictures on the covers of the magazine. Get it? Don't mess up your team by trying to be the hero."

Opening the Box

There's a tendency for us all to want to crawl into a box. It's safe, secure, and cozy. Someone might say something like, "Why haven't you gotten more done?" or "Why haven't you been more successful?" We'd all like to be able to say, "It's not my fault. I'm being held back. I'm boxed in." Sometimes the constraints on us are real. Sometimes they're not. Complaining and blaming are the symptoms of someone who likes to play the "I'm boxed in" game. It's like two dinosaurs standing around complaining about all the meteor showers (or about how cold it's getting, if you prefer that theory). The truth is, complaining and blaming aren't going to get them anywhere. They have to learn to adapt or they'll perish. Take a look at Figure 7-1 and let's see what it means to be in the "can-do" box.

An "A" wall is immovable. It's a stone wall. It's set by the fundamental beliefs of top management. Because it's not going to change, it's foolish to go up against an "A" wall. All you'll do is get bloody and bruised. It would be like someone saying, "I don't want to have to submit a budget for next

Figure 7-1. The can-do box.

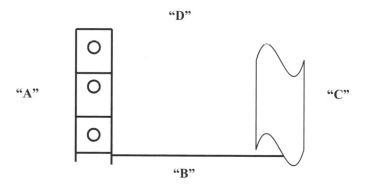

year. I'll just spend whatever I want to." The Golden Rule of Management applies when it comes to "A" walls; those who have the gold make the rules.

A "B" wall is fairly rigid. It's plywood. It can be broken, but you need some help to do it. If you want to deviate from operating guidelines or get policy exceptions, you need someone's approval, and often someone's support, in order to break through a "B" wall. I know some managers who go through their entire career never trying to break through a "B" wall because "they" said things had to be done that way.

A "C" wall looks solid but it isn't. It's like a rubber sheet. You can push it aside completely by yourself. The problem is, many people see it there and they don't want to push. It would be like the person in the high hurdles race saying, "Something's in my way. I can't finish the race." An example in a work situation would be a manager saying, "I'm not going to engineering on this matter. It's their job to come to us."

A "D" wall is the most interesting of them all. It's not even there. It's all in our minds. It's based on assumptions and rumors. To create management magic, you have to work at dispelling the organization myths that hold people back. The following cases represent three sample conversations I've actually had with people in different companies.

Case 1: It's No Use Trying Anything New

Me: What are some things that keep you from getting your job done?

Employee: Well, it's no use trying anything new around here. It's just not allowed.

Me: How do you know that?

Employee: Well, you don't see many new things tried around here.

Me: Have you tried something different, or have you seen someone else try to introduce something new?

Employee: Well, I've never tried it myself because I know what would happen. Others have tried it, though.

Me: How did things turn out for them?

Employee: Fine, but they were taking a huge risk.

Case 2: The Boss Will Punish You If You Don't Know Everything

Me: If you could change anything you wanted around here, what would it be?

Employee: I would cut out all the detailed records you have to keep.

Me: What do you have to do that?

Employee: Around here, you have to have every fact at your fingertips or you'd get in trouble with the boss. He'll really give it to you if you couldn't answer every question you're asked.

Me: Who has gotten in trouble for not having everything at his fingertips?

Employee: A guy in accounting really got clobbered for not knowing the answer to something.

Me: When did that happen?

Employee: Oh, about fifteen years ago.

Me: Has your boss asked you for information you didn't immediately have?

Employee: Oh, sure.

Me: What happened to you?

Employee: Nothing, really. I was lucky.

Case 3: Don't Ask Questions

Me: What could be changed to help you to be more effective at your job?

Employee: Make it possible to ask questions.

Me: You mean you can't ask questions?

Employee: Absolutely not. You don't want to look stupid around here. So, you learn to play the game and act like you understand. That's just the way it is.

Me: Is that what your boss wants people to do?

Employee: She says she wants people to challenge things, to criticize, and to look at all sides of an issue. She claims she welcomes questions. We all know she doesn't mean it.

Me: Does anyone ever ask questions or raise controversial issues?

Employee: Sometimes.

Me: What happens to them?

Employee: Nothing, really. But they're taking a big chance. You won't catch me doing it.

Although paying people competitively is important, outstanding managers know the greatest good we can do for others is not really to share our riches, but to reveal theirs. It's about helping people become something more tomorrow than they are today. A lot of that has to do with helping people to realize the ability they have to do significant things. They can't fall into the trap of spending their time complaining and wishing things were different than they are. They've got to accept that "what is, is" and make the most of it. They can't wait for "more authority" or "clearer direction" or "more control." They've got to act now before they develop the dread disease called "hardening of the attitudes" complicated by "stinking thinking!"

The Forgotten Skill of Listening

Begin really listening to employees on your first day of work, and do it every day thereafter. Real listening is not just waiting for your turn to talk. It's understanding the *meaning* of what someone is trying to say. People always communicate at two levels—what they say and what they mean. "What they say" is the level most managers pay attention to, if they pay attention at all. For instance, the employee says, "Congratulations on the promotion. I know you worked *so* hard to get it." Unfortunately, the comment is dripping with sarcasm. The manager is totally oblivious to the real meaning and says, "Thank you." Or I ask my wife what's wrong and she says in an angry tone, "Nothing!" Or I ask someone how their project is going and they say dejectedly, "Oh, just great!" Real listening is paying attention to the subtext, to the vocal element of the way something is said, and to nonverbals. It's a lot to ask of someone to actually listen, but it's a great opportunity for a manager who wants to be better. What's the number-one answer I get when I ask employees what their manager could do better? You got it. It's listening. (The same thing applies, of course, to husbands and wives, parents and children, and anyone else you can think of.)

In this sense, employees are like customers. They deserve to be treated with respect. The number-one way to treat people with respect is to listen to what they have to say. You can't always give them what they want. But you can always listen to them. Managers are often unskilled communicators, particularly when listening is involved. They fail to ask simple, commonsense questions such as, "What do you think?" or "Does this make sense to you?" or "How do you think it should be done?"

Why are people so bad at listening? I've got to believe it's the way we're brought up. The other communication skills are talking, reading, and writing. Think of how young we are when we're taught those things and how many years in school we have of emphasizing those things. That isn't to say people shouldn't be taught to be better talkers, readers, or writers. Yet, when are people taught to listen? How many years in school do we have of emphasizing it? The answer is that people aren't taught to listen, and there is virtually no instruction in listening. We also don't learn good listening skills from our managers because the odds are they aren't good listeners. I've got to believe that listening is the forgotten skill. Here are a few tips for becoming a better listener:

• Don't multitask. If you are going to listen, then listen. Give the person your undivided attention.

• If you're busy or distracted, tell the other person that it isn't a good time and reschedule the meeting.

• Take notes. It shows the other person you're taking them seriously and helps you recall the conversation.

• Periodically summarize what the other person is saying to you. It teaches you to listen and checks your comprehension.

• Try to be open-minded and not anticipate what the other person is going to say.

• Pay attention to the way someone says something and to the other person's nonverbals. Dr. Albert Mehrabian, in his book, *Silent Messages,* divided communication into three components. He found that the verbal element (the words) accounted for only 7 percent of the meaning, whereas the vocal element (the way the words are said) accounted for 38 percent of the meaning and the nonverbal or visual element (the body language) accounted for 55 percent of the meaning. No wonder e-mail is such a limited form of communication. It's great for confirming agreements and follow-up, but terrible for topics that are controversial or have strong emotions involved.

It's also critical not to give unsolicited advice. The problem is that managers have been rewarded their whole lives for being problem-solvers. For many, it's all they know how to do. I know a lot of managers reading the title of this chapter will assume that "building capability and accountability" would be about telling employees what they should do. They wouldn't assume the opposite—that it's about listening to what employees want to do and asking questions to help them structure the details. When employees start to tell managers about a problem, many managers get impatient and want to fix it immediately. They impose their solution by saying, "Here's what you should do." The manager thinks she has done a great job and the employee vows never to bring up an issue with the manager again. It's insulting and demeaning to be told what to do when the person doesn't even understand the issue. Imagine if my wife came home from work and said, "What a bad day I had today," and I immediately said, "You ought to quit that stupid job of yours. You're always complaining." I don't think she'd be too happy with me. What she wanted was a sympathetic ear. She wanted me to show interest in what she had to say. She wanted me to ask her questions and empathize with her plight. I told her what to do. It implies that I'm smarter and know more than she does about her situation. I've belittled her in the process. I've discounted her and insulted her. No wonder she'd get angry with me. It's quite another thing, of course, when advice is solicited. If my wife said, "What do you think I should do?" then offering an opinion would be very appropriate.

Keeping Discussions Positive

Am I saying you should listen to everything that people have to say? Absolutely not! One of the important things that outstanding managers do is get their people to focus on positive things. Too many groups spend too much time complaining about things they can't do anything about. They lose focus. As a leader, you need to have strong conviction that you want

time and energy spent in a useful way. You must express that to your people as often as necessary, saying in no uncertain terms things like, "Look,
we've got a lot of work to do. We're not going to waste time talking about
that." You set the ground rules. That's your job.

Figure 7-2 is a classic diagram (usually called the "locus of control")
that illustrates what I'm talking about. Just like in baseball before the
game, you review what's in bounds and out of bounds. When something is
out of bounds, you have to be like an umpire and shout "Foul!" Things in
the inner circle—"what we can control"—are always suitable topics. You
and your people want to discuss methods and process improvements constantly. Tell your employees to bring up these issues in meetings or one-on-
one with you. These are things that you can authorize on your own without
getting anyone else's permission. Things in the middle circle—"what we

Figure 7-2. Locus of control.

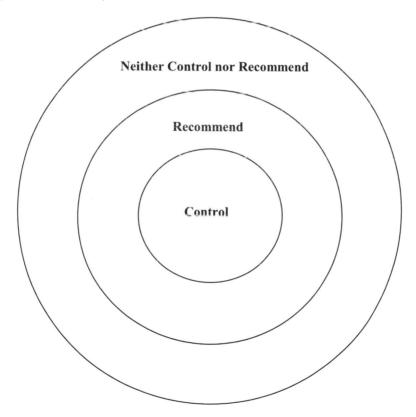

Neither Control nor Recommend

Recommend

Control

can recommend"—may be suitable topics. These are new policies and procedures or changes to existing ones. Typically, you would encourage people to bring these issues to you and then you'd decide whether it's worth pursuing with those you work for or those in other organizations. Things in the outermost circle—"what we can neither control nor recommend"—are taboo. They're not a good use of anyone's time.

I've had many managers ask me, "What can I do with the person who is constantly backstabbing and whining about other people?" The answer is simple—tell them to stop. Get them to agree that they are going to stop and then hold them accountable for what they agreed to. Remember, you're in charge. You set the rules for your organization. If someone doesn't want to follow the rules, then they can't play the game. Outstanding managers have a soft side. They are supportive, caring, and responsive to the needs of their people. They are protective of their employees. They also have a hard side. Don't pander to employees. Don't let them take advantage of you. You're not there to be their friend. The simplest way I can say it is, "Don't take any crap from anyone." You have to have the courage to discipline people who don't do what they agree to do.

The Importance of Delegation

Delegation is the transfer of responsibility for a specific task from you to one of your employees. It can either be a one-time or a continuing responsibility. This means that you'll depend on the employee to handle that task and meet the required performance standards. Sounds easy, doesn't it? It isn't! When you delegate, you must make sure the employee thoroughly understands the new responsibility and has the knowledge and ability to successfully handle the new task. For instance, many parents have had the experience of teaching a child to ride a bike. You can't progress too fast. You hold the handlebars, put on training wheels, and walk alongside the bike. A child typically will say, "You won't let go, will you?" You say, "Of course not. Not until you're ready." Delegation has to be done the same way. You've got to hold the handlebars, put on training wheels, and walk alongside the bike while your employees learn to ride. It is irresponsible for you to just push them down the hill before they're ready. They'll crash and you'll be to blame.

Often, we just take for granted that the other person understands what we want. Let's use another example of a child. You tell your child to go and clean her room, but she gets distracted. You say, "That's it! Get up there now! I'm coming up to inspect and that room had better be clean!" After a minute or two of cleaning, the child says, "Okay, I'm done." No way," you scream, "You couldn't have done it that quickly." The child insists that she has. You go upstairs to inspect and bellow, "You call this clean? This isn't clean. You lied to me!" The child starts to cry and says, "I did, too, clean it." What's the issue here? You never defined specifically what you wanted. You just assumed the child knew what a "clean room" was. It's likely you never gave the child a checklist or detailed explanation of what you expected. That happens in your organization every day. People assume that others know what they have in mind. They might ask, "Do you understand?" People typically say "Yes!" whether they really understand or not. They don't want to look stupid. A better thing to ask would be, "Can you give me a detailed explanation of what you're going to do?"

What's in it for you to delegate?

• *You can devote more time to important management matters because some of your other functions will be handled by your employees.* Most managers feel that they don't have enough time to perform all their job functions. By delegating work, you'll be able to devote more time to those matters that require your attention.

• *You can challenge and motivate employees.* Many talented employees feel underutilized. Assigning challenging responsibilities to them will often bring about increased interest in the job. Many times, these employees show enthusiasm and ability that previously had not been apparent.

• *You can develop employees and make them more valuable.* Additional responsibility may increase an employee's value. New job responsibilities provide additional job experience and training and enable the employee to contribute more. Just feeling more valuable to the organization can be motivating.

There are some clues that can lead you to ideas for things you can delegate. Answer the following questions and you'll see what I mean:

- What are the tasks I do because I like to do them?
- What are the tasks I held on to when I was last promoted?
- What are the tasks I do that have become routine for me, but that my employees could do?
- What are the tasks that I used to like to do, but no longer find interesting or challenging?
- What are the tasks that cause me to work long hours?
- What are the tasks that my employees ask me to do for them?
- What are the tasks that I would delegate if I had more confidence in the skill level of my staff?
- What are the tasks that usually pile up in my absence?

Getting Employee Commitment

A good way to get delegation ideas is directly from your employees. Certainly if they can ask for something, they're much more likely to receive an assignment in a positive frame of mind. The ideal way to delegate is to be able to say something like, "You mentioned that you wanted to get more visibility with top management. I've got a project that will do just that for you." Much better than saying, "I'd like to have you do this project for me."

We've all rented cars before. No one has ever changed the oil, done a tune-up, or rotated the tires on a rental. Why? There's no ownership involved. It's someone else's car. While there's no guarantee, there's certainly a greater likelihood that you'll take care of your own car. You want to make assignments that give employees a feeling of complete responsibility and not just a feeling that they're doing a task for you.

You also want them to use their ingenuity. So many managers get hung up on the fact that they might have more experience or technical know-how, or they think they're smarter than the people who work for them. They think they can do it better. That's only half of the equation, though. Let's say you can do something that's a 94 on a 100-point scale of being right, and your employee can do it only at an 84 level. It might appear that you should have the person do it your way. But, in addition to the rightness of the decision, there's a second consideration called "commitment." Your 94 could be multiplied by, say, 10 percent in employee commitment. Letting someone do it their way at 84 could be multiplied by a 90 percent in commitment. Both rightness and commitment carry equal weight. But look at Figure 7-3. Letting someone who has the ability do it their way is usually a better deal. You don't have to know much about math to know that if something is done totally wrong with 100 percent commitment, the product result will be zero. On the other hand, even if something is 100 percent right and there's zero commitment, you'll get a zero result in the end. That's why it's common to see great ideas fail and mediocre ideas succeed. Commitment is a key ingredient. So, what's the lesson? Be very specific on the end results needed. Make sure your employees understand them. But, if it's at all possible, let them come up with the way to get the task accomplished.

The Reluctant Employee

When an employee is asked to accept a new responsibility, he may want to think it over before giving you a commitment. It's not unusual for someone to say, "I'm sorry, but I can't do that. I've never done anything like it before. No thanks." Then, the person comes back the next day and says, "You know, I've been thinking about it. That thing you wanted me to do. It would be a real challenge. I was scared off at first. Is it still available?" This is likely to happen if the new responsibility seems extremely challenging or the employee feels he already has too much to do. You may pay a price in lack of commitment if you force the responsibility on the employee. Instead, ask the employee to think it over and agree on a specific time when the two of you can meet again to discuss the task. Be sure to emphasize the reasons you're asking the employee to take on the new responsibility.

It's often helpful to remind employees of challenges met and new responsibilities they have successfully taken on in the past. If necessary, you

Figure 7-3. Balancing rightness and commitment.

Rightness	Commitment	Result
94	10%	940
84	90%	7,560
100	0%	0
0	100%	0

can ask employees to do you a favor and take on the new responsibility because it would mean a lot to you and the organization. Be sure to express appreciation now, and again later, for their willingness to help out.

If people are reluctant to take on new assignments, it really helps if you tell them why you're choosing them for the assignment and can review their recent accomplishments. For instance, if you can say, "I'm asking you to do this because you're the best we've got at negotiating agreements," that kind of sincere flattery goes a long way. Don't make it up. It's got to be real. Then follow up with a specific example, if possible: "You were the one who took on that extremely difficult Alpha project. No one thought you'd be able to pull it off, yet you did. And how about the work you did on Beta? That was amazing." You can and should make it awfully difficult for someone to say "No" to you. Do it through praise and specific facts. Don't ever do it through threats or intimidation.

The Four Key Questions

There are four key questions to ask when giving someone a work assignment. Most managers, interestingly enough, ask none of the four questions:

1.   *Will you do it?* Amazingly, most managers just say, "Here's what I want you to do," or "Do me a favor," and they never ask for a commitment. To significantly increase the likelihood that the person will actually do what you're asking, get the person to say out loud that she will do it. Don't just assume she will. Also, if the employee says something like, "I'll try," then respond the way Master Yoda did in *The Empire Strikes Back.* Yoda asked Luke Skywalker to levitate the spaceship out of the swamp. Luke made the mistake of saying, "I'll try." Yoda responded just the way a good manager should: "There is no try. There is only do. Do or not do." So, like Yoda, don't accept any "maybes."

2.   *How will you do it?* It's one thing to agree you're going to do something and quite another to put together a plan on how you're going to accomplish it. A good manager will always ask for an action plan. Many managers have foolish, worthless conversations. "I need you to cut down on your errors," the manager will say. The employee says, "Okay, I'll try to do better." The manager says, "Good. I'm glad we had this little talk."

That talk was worth nothing. A smarter manager will say, "What exactly are you going to do differently?"

3. *What could prevent you from doing it?* Excuses after the fact aren't worth anything. But, before the fact, they're very useful. Ask the employee all the things that could go wrong. If he doesn't know, have him talk to those who have worked on similar projects or assignments. Have employees give you all the excuses for failure before they even start on the task.

4. *What could you do to overcome that problem?* For each of the excuses, have employees think through what they could do to take preventive action. If the preventive action doesn't work, then ask them what they could do to get back on track. Very early in my career, I thought my job was to get my manager's approval to do something and then get out of his office as quickly as possible. I would be barely out the door when things would start to go wrong. That's the way life is. Murphy had it right: "If anything can go wrong, it will." My people would say, "What do we do now?" I'd have to say, "I don't know. Let me talk to my boss." Wasted time! But I got a little smarter and began to say to my boss, "These are all the things that I think are likely to go wrong, and these are the actions I'd like to take if these things do, in fact, go wrong." That way, I got advance approval and was empowered to take a variety of actions. I'd be barely out of my manager's office when my people would tell me things were going wrong, only now I'd immediately be able to tell them what to do. They'd say, "Don't you need approval to deviate from plan?" I'd say, "Don't worry about it. It's taken care of." What a difference!

The best managers are devoted to two things—meeting the needs of the organization and meeting the needs of their employees. To do just one of these things is not being a complete manager. To do neither one of these things puts you in the category of taking up space and not really having any added value. To do both of these things makes you invaluable to your organization. You're never done with the effort since the needs of the organization and the needs of its employees are constantly changing. But, if you're good, you walk the tightrope and somehow never fall off.

It's About Time!

Your life is crazy, isn't it? It's getting crazier all the time. Just too much to do and too little time to do it. Your personal life is just like your work life. It's a roller-coaster. It's always been that way, but it seems the roller-coaster is getting steeper, the curves more and more frequent, and there aren't any more straightaways where you can relax. Well, you're not alone. The truth is, the only person who got everything done by Friday was . . . Robinson Crusoe!

You've got to come to grips with the fact that you can't get it all done. You can't be all things to all people. If you try, you'll be like a juggler attempting to juggle forty-seven balls in the air at the same time. You'll drop them all. You'll never be praised and rewarded for attempting to do many things. You'll only be praised and rewarded for what you successfully complete. So, concentrate on the few important things. Get them accomplished.

It Takes Courage

Remember the discipline you had in school? You'd always want to know if something was going to be on the exam. If so, you'd study it. If not, you learned to let it go. Work is just like that. If it's important, do it. If not, let it go. There are too many people who go around saying, "I can't get to the big, important things because the little day-to-day things keep getting in the way." It takes courage to say, "Wait a minute. It's the big, important things that matter. I should do them first. If I have time left over, then I should do the little day-to-day things." Why don't people work that way? They're afraid. Afraid of getting in trouble. Ironically, because they do the little things first and don't get to the big things, they *do* get in trouble. They spend their time on tasks inversely related to their importance. People exhibit a lot of characteristics at work. Unfortunately, courage is not usually one of them.

We've got all kinds of electronic gadgets to help us become better organized. Unfortunately, they often add more clutter to our already-cluttered lives. These things may help us to be more efficient, but they don't address the real issue—*efficient doing what?* We need to take a penetrating look at how we spend our time instead of just saving it to waste it again.

The Four Steps

Here's a four-step process that every manager at every level in every organization should follow.

1. *Concentrate on what's important.* Decide on what's meaningful and eliminate the distractions that keep you from pursuing it. An obvious point, yes, but most of us fail to do it. Instead, we busy ourselves with trivia. A good rule of thumb is to stop doing the unimportant things you have time to do and start doing the few important things you don't have time to do.

We could all benefit from the counsel of Henry David Thoreau, who wrote *Walden* in 1854. His vision of personal choice applies as easily to the twenty-first century as it did to his pre–Industrial Revolution world. Thoreau said it elegantly: "Simplicity, simplicity, simplicity! I say, let your affairs be as two or three, and not a hundred or a thousand; instead of a million count half a dozen, and keep your accounts on your thumbnail."

2. *Question everything you do.* How much of your job is devoted to ritual and routine tasks that are of questionable importance? If you find yourself working harder and getting less and less done, this may be at least part of the problem. Stripping away these extraneous things can be a painful process. It takes clear thinking and relentless hard work. It's kind of like cleaning out the attic. If you don't need it, get rid of it! Keep asking

why you have to do something until you discover if a specific task is necessary. Unless you're willing to keep going until you find an answer, you'll keep performing activities rather than producing results.

How many bureaucratic procedures, reports, meetings, and other activities go on in your department because you've "always done them that way." Question them all. Once you're done, question them again. Get in the habit of thinking like an outsider and looking at your job as if you're seeing it for the first time. Something that was appropriate one month may be inappropriate the next. Constantly ask yourself and your staff what tasks could be pruned. If you must add a procedure, meeting, or new task, try to take an old one away. Everyone knows it's good to have a to-do list of activities each day. It's probably better to have a not-to-do list of activities each day.

Early in my career, I was naïve. I thought busy people *must* be doing important things. I can remember a savvy manager telling me that he wanted to get a do-nothing operations manager out of the way. So, he made him a "special assistant" and told him he would handle special projects. Only there were no special projects. A few weeks later, I can remember going into the operations manager's office late one night. He had charts and graphs all over his office. I asked him how the job was going. He said it was great; he had never been busier or happier. He was going from one meeting to another, offering his "special" assistance. I learned a valuable lesson: You don't have to be doing anything to feel busy.

Thoreau was talking about nations, but he could have easily been talking about companies when he described them as ". . . an unwieldy and overgrown establishment, cluttered with furniture and tripped up by its own traps, ruined by luxury and heedless expense, by want of calculation and a worthy aim . . . ."

3. *Stop time-robbers.* The chief duties of many managers involve nothing more than completing plans, communicating results, reporting on why results did *not* meet plans, reporting on why results *did* meet plans, summarizing results, and summarizing summaries. How useful are these activities? Or, rather, how much do these activities cost the organization? Isn't it interesting that when a company eliminates layers and layers of management, its stock price immediately shoots up. Wall Street is smart. A little less bureaucracy is good for an organization. Wall Street knows that

the role of too many managers has become one of trying to please those they work for and irritating those who work for them.

These managers surround themselves—suffocate themselves—with electronics that are attached to and hanging off their bodies like parasites. They talk into invisible microphones. Some of them boast proudly of the thousand e-mails they get each day and how they have no time to open them, let alone read them. They go from one conference call to another. They're so addicted to their BlackBerrys that they might as well be called "CrackBerrys." They multitask themselves, and their departments, to an early grave. Thoreau was a prophet when he said: "Men have become the tools of their tools. . . . Our inventions are wont to be pretty toys, which distract our attention from serious things."

4. *Don't ask permission.* Anyone at any level can make positive change. Unfortunately, many people feel they don't have the authority to make those changes. I can't tell you how many people have said in seminars, "That's a great idea, but my boss will never go for it." I usually say, "Why in the world do you want to talk to your boss about it? Just go do it." The idea of taking action is frightening to many managers. It takes courage. How many acts of courage do you see in your organization in a typical day? Probably not enough. People also love to say, "It's got to start at the top." What exactly has to start at the top? "If I'm going to improve my effectiveness, it's got to start at the top," the manager says. What could be more ridiculous than that? It's just another excuse for nonaction. That's like saying, "If I'm going to be more effective in my job, it's got to start with the president of the United States and his Cabinet."

I remember a situation where there seemed to be no good reason for a particularly cumbersome procedure, so I stopped it. The vice president I worked for found out about it and exclaimed, "How dare you change procedures without my permission! Who gave you the authority to do that?" I told him I stopped the report two years before and no one seemed to notice. He said, "Oh. Okay, then. No problem." I was off the hook because I didn't ask permission. If I had asked first, I never would have been able to do it.

Very few people ever get in trouble for becoming more effective and productive. Be a role model for everyone else. Get outstanding performance reviews. That's the only real protection you'll ever have. Become invaluable to your organization. Then you've got the autonomy you need. Don't be run by the mindless bureaucracy, because then you'll be part of the problem and not part of the solution.

This is the kind of mental toughness that Thoreau was suggesting when he wrote: "No way of thinking or doing, however ancient, can be trusted without proof. What everybody echoes or in silence endorses as true today may turn out to be falsehood tomorrow, mere smoke of opinion. . . . Old deeds for old people, and new deeds for new."

Let me further illustrate these points with a personal story: I can remember sitting in on the first staff meeting of a vice president of marketing. His group had a terrible reputation. They were known to be long on promises but short on delivery. He asked the 125 people what they were working on. He couldn't believe all the projects. He started to write them on a whiteboard. Soon the board was completely full. "Well, which of these is the most important?" he asked. "Everything's a hot priority around this place," shouted one of his people. He had heard enough. On the spot, he came up with a "degrees of hotness" system. White hot was terribly important, red hot the next most important, and so on. He forced them to prioritize. Only five projects made it to the highest category—white hot. He told everyone to stop whatever they were working on and assigned them to five project teams. Within a few weeks, people around the company were marveling at the fact that the marketing people had finally gotten focused. They talked about the huge "turnaround" by this group. The vice president understood exactly what we were talking about. Left to their own devices, people will do a little bit of a lot of things and not have much to show for it in the end.

The Work-Planning Pyramid

Approach time management the way you would any business issue. It's all about coming up with a plan and then executing the plan. When things take you off course, either get back on plan or revise your plan. Start big and then work your way down the "work-planning pyramid," as illustrated in Figure 8-1.

Figure 8-1. The work-planning pyramid.

Start with your vision of what you want to accomplish by the end of the week, month, year, and lifetime. You can't decide how to get somewhere if you don't know where you're going. Your personal vision can change from time to time. No problem. Then, plan on the goals that will help make that vision a reality.

Every goal should be divided into short-term activities. It may take a hundred activities to accomplish one of your goals. Each of the activities will take time, so you need to schedule them in. Too much work? You know the old expression, "If you fail to plan, you're planning to fail." What's your choice? To be driven by events? Wouldn't you rather drive events? See what happens? Play it by ear? Those aren't the things that take-charge people say. It's doubly tough on you. As a manager, you have to be terrific at the difficult things we're talking about and then also teach your people to do them. The best way to teach, of course, is to be a role model. Teach by your actions.

The Time-Management Matrix

So, what's the best use of your time? Let's take a look at the time-management matrix in Figure 8-2.

Most people's jobs are dominated by Quadrant I activities—those activities that are important and seem nondiscretionary. You "have to do" the fire-fighting. You are stressed by deadline-driven projects and con-

Figure 8-2. Time-management matrix.

	Nondiscretionary	Discretionary
Important	**I** Fire-fighting Deadline-driven projects Problems Crises	**II** Relationship building Process improvement Planning Coaching and developing others
Not Important	**III** Phone calls Meetings E-mail Drop-in visitors	**IV** "Retained hobbies" Passing information Bureaucracy Monkeys

sumed by problems, and you handle one crisis after another. Right? That's what everyone around you is doing. That's your "culture." The problem with only doing Quadrant I activities is that they're reactive. You respond to issues. It's kind of like shoveling sand against the tide. You work hard, but you don't really get anywhere.

The way to cut into Quadrant I is to invest in Quadrant II activities. They are also important, but they're discretionary, so most people don't spend much time on them. Some managers spend no time on them at all. They include building relationships, implementing process improvement so things are made easier, planning, and coaching and developing others. These are proactive activities. You invest in these activities. They pay off later for you. That's why people put off doing them.

Quadrant III activities seem nondiscretionary, but the key is that you define them as nonimportant or, at least, of lesser importance. You have to deal with certain phone calls, meetings, e-mail, and drop-in visitors. You can't ever eliminate these things entirely. But you can spend less time on them. For example, you're asked to give a fifteen-minute presentation as part of a two-hour meeting. Most people will sit through the entire two hours. Maybe they'll get to you. Often, they won't and you'll have to come back next time. A good time manager will say, "Could we do my presentation for the first fifteen minutes? I'd appreciate that." Some of the time, at least, the meeting planner will say, "Sure, no problem." That's the kind of thing I'm talking about. A little thing that can potentially save you a lot of time.

Quadrant IV activities are the most interesting of them all. They're discretionary and unimportant. You'd think people would never do them. But some people are overwhelmed by them. They're things like "retained hobbies," passing information, dealing with bureaucracy, and "monkeys."

What's a "retained hobby"? I once knew a vice president who was extremely busy. He worked lots of hours and raced around all the time. He complained that he had little time to devote to strategic planning, building relationships with other executives, and spearheading programs that would improve the organization. Once I began to observe him, however, I noticed how much time he spent on tasks that weren't part of his job. For example, he had an old-fashioned drafting board in his office. Both he and his drafting board were antiques. He worked on plant layouts and production-line changes. He was doing work that should have been done three or more levels below him in the organization using modern technology. Why was he doing it? He had been a draftsman and had worked his way up through the engineering ranks. He was continuing to do the things he was comfortable in doing—his "retained hobbies"—instead of doing the things he should have been doing. He managed to keep so busy doing the former that he had no time to do the latter. The truth is, he wasn't very comfortable with strategic planning, building relationships with other executives, and spearheading programs that would improve the organization. He conveniently avoided those things by filling his days and nights with retained hobbies. Many managers are like that vice president. They spend their time on tasks inversely related to their importance.

What about avoiding bureaucracy and passing information from one person to another? I once worked with someone who spent two and a half days of every week preparing a routine report. I asked her why she did the report, a question she obviously had never asked herself. Her response: "It's a very important report. Look at how many people receive copies of it." There were, in fact, twenty-six names on the recipient list, but I still didn't know *why* she did the report. "I'll get in trouble if I don't do it," she said. I told her to contact the twenty-six people and ask them if they considered the report critically important. Reluctantly, she went along with my request. How many of those twenty-six people indicated that the report was critically important? None of them. We eliminated the report and gained twenty hours per week of her time.

The term "monkeys" was coined by William Oncken. It refers to passing action items or problems from one person to another. If you're not careful, someone can come in to your office and say, "Boss, I need your help. I don't know what to do." It's not unusual for a manager to then "take the monkey off the back" of that person by responding, "Don't worry about it. I'll take care of it." You've played hero and the employee has played helpless. The employee is rewarded with one less problem to worry about and you're punished with one more problem to worry about. If you're not careful, you can spend your day collecting monkeys. You'll be known as a bottleneck because you won't be able to get "your job" done. In truth, "your job" now consists of the things that everyone else doesn't want to do. Sound familiar? It's very easy to see at home. If you continually tell your kids, "I want you to clean your room," and they don't do it, the worst thing to do is to clean it for them. You're teaching them irresponsible behavior. You're also creating a lot more work for yourself. The lesson? Your employees should be cleaning their own rooms.

There's no such thing as not having enough time. We've all got the same amount. It's twenty-four hours in a day and 168 hours in a week. That's all the hours there are. There'll never be any more. Make the most of them!

Action Items for Developing Your Ability to Plan and Organize Your Group's Performance

Planning/Organizing Your Group's Performance—Defining, organizing, and scheduling work requirements in order to appropriately assign tasks, secure commitment, allocate resources, and monitor progress toward desired outcomes.

• Get clarity from your manager on what the specific expectations are for you and your department for the coming quarter, six months, and year, so that you can focus your efforts appropriately. Ask for performance targets that have quantitative measures.

• Together with those who assign you work, develop a method for sorting requests according to their priority. After using the method for a while, check back to make any needed changes.

• Before starting a task or assignment, ask yourself what could go wrong. Plan and take steps to prevent potential problems.

• Break down larger activities into smaller, more manageable steps. Set milestones and deadlines for each step to keep yourself on track and to help mark each accomplishment that moves you closer to the achievement of your larger goals.

• Be able to define how your work is measured and assessed. Make sure your definitions are in line with those of your manager.

• Determine ahead of time a way to reward yourself for accomplishing a key goal or objective (e.g., decide that you will have lunch at a good restaurant).

• Ask your manager to explain the broader business context of a project or assignment so that you know how what you are being asked to do contributes to the company's overall business objectives. Use this knowledge to determine how you'll measure the outcome of your work.

• Take courses in time management, project management, and project planning to learn about tools and techniques you can use to schedule, organize, and prioritize your work effectively.

• Learn about and use existing resources (e.g., people, tools, systems, processes) that can help you track and measure your progress on projects and assignments.

• When developing project plans, take into consideration your other work commitments. Map out a timetable and set expectations that are challenging but realistic and achievable, given other work obligations or project demands.

• Set goals with short-term steps to give yourself a sense of achievement as you work toward accomplishing the bigger and broader objectives.

• Develop a time-management system that is flexible enough to allow you to reprioritize your work as demands change, so your attention remains focused on accomplishing the most important activities first.

• Observe peers in other work groups who are known for getting results. Note what processes and/or systems they use and adopt those that seem appropriate for your department or work group.

• At the beginning of the week or month, choose an issue that has been causing you frustration and that you've been meaning to address. Plan and write out what steps you'll take to move it to resolution.

Driving Results Through
Your Organization

Managing Employee Performance

Management takes pride in producing state-of-the-art products, services, and support systems. Yet most companies are woefully lacking in the most basic, fundamental management system—the performance management process. They have archaic, worn-out programs that were designed for a different generation. They simply do not work anymore.

The Problem with Performance Reviews

For most managers and employees, the performance review is like two porcupines in love—it's a pain for both parties. (However, if you want little porcupines . . . I guess that's a different book. We won't get into that here.) Many performance reviews do more harm than good. They don't help the boss-employee relationship. They hurt it. They do not improve employee morale. They decrease it. They breed mistrust and create barriers to effective working relationships. Performance reviews have probably done more harm to employee morale than any invention since the layoff. In traditional performance review systems, managers are forced to make subjective judgments on an employee's personality, psychological makeup, and intentions. They cannot explain or defend these judgments. Neither side benefits.

Often a review is a "but-but" experience. That doesn't refer to a part of the anatomy. It means the manager is the attacker and the employee is the defender. It tests the employee's stamina. The employee starts sentences with the word *but*: "But you didn't tell me," and "But I assumed," and "But you said," and "But this is the first I've heard of it," and "But I had no idea." Most employees give up after a few "but-but" sentences and say, "Okay, whatever you want. Let's just get this over with." They're reluctantly compliant the rest of the way. The manager says, "I guess I convinced them." Then they go out and unload on other employees who sympathize with their plight, knowing their time is coming.

As students, we were given objective exams, then we were graded on our papers, had midterm tests, and took final exams. We knew how we were doing all semester long. In the work world, you're subject to the awful process of being kept in the dark for a year and then being victim of the dreaded (a drum roll would be appropriate here) performance review. People look forward to the review about as much as they look forward to a root canal. It's like an athlete in training for a race turning to the coach and saying, "Coach, you've got the stopwatch. How fast did I run?" The coach responds, "I'll let you know next year at your performance review." Then, the athlete says, "Coach, don't I deserve to know? How will I improve?" The coach says, "Look, if I had any problems with your performance, I'd let you know." Sound familiar? How are you going to turn out dedicated athletes that way?

Managers are uncomfortable with the performance review process. They delay it as long as they can and try to get through it as quickly as possible. They typically apologize to employees for having to subject them to the review and blame the whole mess on the human resources department.

During performance reviews, employees usually feel defenseless and taken advantage of. In another age, it was considered natural for people to feel that way. The typical employee response was, "Yes, sir. Whatever you say. Can I go now?" (And it was mostly "sir" back then.) These days, many employees will try to give their version of what really happened, so it becomes a "but-but" review, with the employee saying, "But that's not the way things happened."

Typical Dialogue

Employees today are more astute, more aware of their rights, and have more mobility. They ask hard questions like, "What are you talking about?" Of course, some choose not to ask questions. They simply post their resume on the Internet and leave the company. A typical performance review dialogue is often an awkward, difficult experience for the manager as well as the employee. Here's a typical exchange:

Manager: I rate you "below average" in versatility [or any of the other murky behavior characteristics found on check-off-the-box forms].

Employee: I don't understand. Below average in relation to whom or what? How have you measured the versatility of everyone else? What is *versatility,* anyhow? We have gone an entire year and this is the first time you have used that word. If it's so important, why haven't you mentioned it until today?

Manager: I'm not sure what they mean by it. It's here on the form and I have to check it off. I'm not sure what any of these things mean. I'm sorry. I've been so busy. Let's just get this over with. So, I rate you average in citizenship. Your teamwork needs improvement. Pretty good in your work habits . . .

Employee: Look. I can appreciate the fact that you have problems, but why should I be penalized for that? If you had any issues with my performance, why didn't you tell me? Why wait until now when it's too late to do anything about it?

Manager: I'm sorry. It won't happen again. I should have talked to you about it before.

Employee: That's what you told me last year. And the year before that. And the year before that.

Clearly, the deck is stacked against the manager with the old-fashioned performance review. Employees may not actually *say* the words the employee said in the example. They *think* them, though. Worse still, many performance reviews are late. My daughter, Lori, has a birthday on March 5. A late performance review is like saying "Happy Birthday" to her on September 5. It sort of loses its punch, doesn't it? I'd compound the oversight if I told her how busy I was and how I didn't have time for her over the last six months. She'd say, "If you don't have time for me, Dad, don't expect me to have time for you." I wouldn't blame her at all!

How to Do It Right

Can this mess be turned into something useful? Yes! It begins with following a logical sequence using up-to-date assumptions about employees. It puts the *performance* back in performance review. It recognizes that employees are adults, not children. They are citizens, voters, and taxpayers. They deserve to be treated as responsible, intelligent, important members of the organization. If a manager expects responsible, adult behavior from an employee, the manager must treat the employee in a responsible, adult manner. A review should be a discussion between two people that *reviews* information. Nothing new should be introduced. Nothing in it should be a surprise. Furthermore, the performance management process should be year-round. There's no way a productive discussion can be held once a year on someone's performance.

Making the process useful takes an understanding of the real purpose of performance reviews. It's to *improve employee performance*. Employees crave recognition and positive reinforcement. They want to feel that their work is recognized and appreciated. Imagine how useful this process would be if an employee went away feeling that the review was a complete, accurate description of actual contributions over the past year. Written praise for past achievements and recognition of special accomplishments are strong motivators for the employee. Instead, as we all know, employees too often say, "The manager doesn't even know what we do." That doesn't stop their managers from giving them their performance reviews, though.

Better Dialogue

Managers should do the performance review *with* and not *for* the employee. Even if a manager had to use a system that talks about behavior characteristics, the dialogue should be something like this:

Manager: The next category is initiative. How would that apply to your job?

Employee: I guess that would mean doing things on my own and not waiting to be asked.

Manager: How do you think you've done on that?

Employee: Okay, I guess. I probably could have done more.

Manager: Such as?

Employee: Well, we've talked about . . .

Three Essential Steps

A good performance management process is made up of three essential steps:

1. *Goal-Setting.* The manager and employee negotiate what has to be accomplished during the performance review period. Goals must be SMART—specific, measurable, achievable, results-oriented, and time-bounded. If annual goals are not practical, then monthly or even weekly goals should be set. The manager and employee should meet for renegotiation as often as necessary. As the employee, knowing what you're supposed to do puts you at a powerful advantage over most people. It used to be that jobs were clearly defined and very straightforward. Accountants, for example, kept the books. They put the debits on the left and the credits on the right. Today, computers do the routine work. We expect our professionals to analyze, influence, persuade, and inform. They have to be clever enough to unravel the mystery of how their success will be measured. Once you know how your performance will be evaluated, you then can intelligently structure your day. So many people, unfortunately, don't know what's important in their job and they can't structure their day. The day structures them. They drift from one thing to another. They go with the flow. And the "you know what" flows downhill.

2. *Progress Reviews.* The manager and employee periodically discuss job performance. The employee brings in action plans for approval, recommends corrective action for problem resolution, and offers ideas for development actions. If the manager has a problem with any area of the employee's performance, this is the time for bringing it up. It should not be saved up for the annual performance review. This way, the manager is helping the employee to remedy the problem before it's documented and viewed by the employee as unfair punishment. If all is going well, this is an ideal time for the manager to give sincere, specific, positive reinforcement. Without praise, employees assume that the manager is only going to pay

attention to them when there are problems. That often gives rise to more problems. This exchange is *not* a progress review:

Manager: How's it going?

Employee: Good.

Manager: Any problems?

Employee: Nothing I can't handle.

Manager: So, I can count on you to get your goals accomplished?

Employee: I'll do the best I can.

Manager: Great. Glad we had this little talk.

This exchange is worth nothing. It's a waste of time. The manager who has vague, pointless discussions like that is going to get some nasty surprises in the end.

3. *Performance Reviews.* No new information is introduced at the annual performance review. The manager and employee should document what has been discussed previously in progress reviews. There should be no forced distribution of performance ratings. This is a bad tradition that serves no purpose. Imagine if I had to rate my four children and the ratings had to fall into a normal distribution, so I was forced to call one of them above average, two of them average, and one of them below average. It would serve no useful purpose. They're *all* wonderful! Why would I want to destroy my relationship with them with such foolishness? I'd have to say the kind of hogwash that many managers do: "I'm sorry, Mindy, but the system requires me to call one of you below average. You're really wonderful, but it's your turn this time. Everyone else has had to take a hit. It's your turn."

Even worse is the practice of "totem ranking," where many organizations rank people in terms of something, but no one quite knows what. Imagine if I had to do a totem ranking of my wife. I'd have to tell her that I rank her forty-second among the sixty-one wives in the neighborhood. Why in the world would I want to do that? Wouldn't she want to know the evaluation criteria? Do you think she might be a little upset with me? Trying to keep the totem ranking a secret makes it seem even more evil. We all know there are no secrets in an organization. Everything comes out in one way or another. Imagine if she said, "I heard you ranked me forty-second out of sixty-one wives. You went around telling everyone else that, but you kept it hidden from me? Is that right?" Do you think when you do similar things to your employees that they might be a little upset with you?

I even know one organization that rates people different colors based on their performance and potential. No one is quite sure what is meant by "potential." That doesn't stop them from calling someone a "blue-red" or a "green-yellow." Worse still, they keep the practice and color combinations a closely guarded secret. How long does it take employees to find out about this "double secret probation" practice? Almost all of them find out about it on their first day of work. That's the day they begin to wonder what other secrets there are around the organization. The biggest problem is that we can't judge anyone's potential. Some people start fast and soon peak, while others are slow in developing and then really take off. I'd rather treat everyone as if they are high potential.

Goal Setting

Many so-called goals are not worth the paper they're printed on. Something like "Learn and grow" or "Improve your relationships with the field organization" or "Continue to work on special projects" doesn't mean anything. All goals should be stated in specific terms that identify precisely what, when, and to what extent something must be done. All goals should be output-oriented (i.e., focused on results) and typically fall into one of three categories:

1. *Routine/Maintenance Goals.* Activities that are repetitive, ongoing, and currently functioning at acceptable levels. These goals do not change present status but seek to maintain it.
2. *Improvement/Problem-Solving Goals.* A problem situation exists that requires a change from X to Y.
3. *Innovation/Creative Goals.* New ideas, new projects, or changes in technology are needed to create something that hasn't existed before.

Be sure not to fall into the trap of discussing salary increases at performance review time. Raises are based on a variety of factors with performance being only one of them—and often not the most important determinant. The other factors are usually job grade, performance of others in the job category, and particular corporate guidelines for the review period. Discussing salary diverts attention from the real issue during the performance review process, which is improving performance. So have separate meetings for the performance review and salary discussion.

Managers who say they don't have time for goal-setting, progress reviews, and performance reviews are saying they don't understand why their job exists. It's like Rembrandt saying he doesn't have time to paint, Einstein saying he's too busy to work with numbers, or Jonas Salk saying he'll invent vaccines someday if he gets around to it. Helping employees succeed is not something managers do only if they have time available after they get their job done. It *is* their job. Anything else is secondary.

Two-Way Communication

During a goal-setting, progress review, or performance review session, the employee should do most of the talking. The managers should ask questions and do a lot of listening. Outstanding managers stress collaborative goals. They are clear about the specific results they want to achieve. They don't speak in terms such as "Do your best" or "See what you can do." They take complex projects and break them down into achievable steps. They actively involve others in planning, giving them as much discretion as possible to make their own decisions. Overall, this isn't just the best way to deal with your employees, it's becoming the only way as employees become smarter and more demanding.

It would be a really good idea if you made giving feedback a two-way process. People appreciate relationships that are give-and-take. A marriage that is only one way—with one giver and one taker—is usually an unhappy one. If you're going to give the employee feedback, as you certainly should, it only seems reasonable that the employee give you some feedback. The wrong way to do this is to ask leading questions. For instance, you won't learn much if you say, "I'm a terrific manager, aren't I?" or "You don't have any problems with me, do you?" Instead, have various ways to get feedback in individual as well as group settings.

One method I've found very useful is called "start, stop, continue." It's simply a form that managers should have their employees fill out periodically. Figure 9-1 is a sample. People typically aren't reluctant to use this method because there's no value judgment—they're not saying anything about your personality or intentions. It's in an objective, action-item format.

Today's employees increasingly aren't accepting a passive role in a process that helps determine their career success. To generate accurate and meaningful reviews of past performance, managers need the perspective of the employee. A self-appraisal should *always* be part of the performance review process. It requires employees to actively participate in their own evaluations. The manager first solicits input from the employee in order to help generate an accurate review. The employee, in turn, gains a better understanding of, and commitment to, the whole review process.

Rather than being pitted against one another in a power struggle, the manager and employee should cooperate to identify the employee's accomplishments. As part of this process, areas needing improvement should be discussed in a constructive manner that emphasizes how results can be better achieved in the future. If the manager focuses on what someone did

Figure 9-1. "Start, stop, continue" feedback form.

What would you like to see me START doing that I'm not doing now?

_____

_____

_____

What would you like to see me STOP doing that I am doing now?

_____

_____

_____

What would you like to make sure I CONTINUE doing?

_____

_____

_____

wrong, it's typically seen as blaming. If the manager focuses on what some-one can do better in the future, it's typically seen as a development discussion and things will go much smoother. Input from other sources should be gathered to increase the accuracy of the review. Objective measures that reflect the subordinate's performance from the perspective of external or internal customers can be particularly valuable.

The manager and employee can choose any appropriate collaborative method to complete the review form. After that, there are several possibilities:

- The employee completes a self-appraisal and the manager then completes a draft of the review form, and they negotiate any differences between the two versions.
- The manager and employee jointly complete the review form together.
- The employee completes a self-appraisal and it is edited by the manager prior to being written in final form.
- The manager completes the review form and the employee self-appraisal is attached to it, with both documents becoming a part of the employee's file.

How to Give a Merit Increase

There's often an uneasy relationship between the human resources department and the managers in an organization. From the HR standpoint, managers don't bother to learn the policies and procedures of the organization. From the managers' standpoint, human resources doesn't explain what those policies and procedures are, or the reasons for them. HR just assumes that managers are supposed to know what they are and how to administer them. It's one of those arguments where both sides are right. At salary increase time, many managers aren't sure of what to say to their employees, so they say nothing. I can remember getting a slightly larger paycheck than usual about a month and a half after my annual merit review was due. I took it to my boss and asked him if he knew anything about it. He said, "Oh, right. You got a raise. I meant to tell you." I considered giving the salary increase back (to be honest with you, though, I didn't consider it for long). What was my boss's job title? VP of Human Resources, of course!

Often managers aren't sure what to say, so they simply make something up like, "Here's your 3 percent raise. I wish it could be more, but that's all they're giving this year." Other times, they try to endear themselves to the employee by saying something like, "I put you in for an 8 percent raise, but the VP knocked it down to 3 percent. You know how he is. There was nothing I could do about it."

So, how should raises be given? I'll wager that no one ever talked to you about that. Remember, have this salary increase discussion after the performance review discussion. Don't try to do it all at once. If you do, the person will only want to know the amount of the salary increase and the rest of the conversation will be of little value.

Assuming you have job grades and ranges in your organization, it's all about midpoint control. If you don't know if you have job grades and ranges, you should find out. A range consists of a minimum, midpoint, and maximum for each grade level. The ranges are usually reviewed once a year in a company, although not necessarily changed. The real value of a job is the midpoint. Individual performance is measured against the midpoint with the "fully competent employee" expected to be paid about that amount. If performance is less than what you'd expect of an employee in that position—for example, because someone is learning the job—pay should be in the lower half of the range. The upper part of the range is reserved for those whose performance is above what you'd expect of an employee in that position. Therefore, employee salaries grow through the range only when performance constantly improves. Salaries level off when performance levels off. When that happens, an employee may get no increase or simply a raise consistent with the amount that the salary range moves. Figure 9-2 is a five-factor performance rating system. It shows why someone who, for example, never moves past "Fully meets requirements" will never move past the midpoint of the range. Someone who gets a zero percent increase would either have to improve his performance or get a promotion to a higher grade level in order to be eligible for a salary increase the next time around.

This commonly used salary matrix considers job performance and position in the salary range. When talking to your employees, show them the matrix and then review job performance by referring to previous performance review discussions and pointing out position in the range. Remember,

Figure 9-2. Five-factor performance review system.

Sample Salary Guidelines

	1st Quartile	2nd Quartile	3rd Quartile	4th Quartile
Far Exceeds	8–10%	6–8%	4–6%	2–4%
Usually Exceeds	6–8%	4–6%	2–4%	0–2%
Fully Meets	4–6%	2–4%	0–2%	0%
Usually Meets	2–4%	0–2%	0%	0%
Below Requirements	0-2%	0%	0%	0%

the worst kind of salary discussion is when the manager doesn't take the time to discuss compensation practices or doesn't have the knowledge to do it. Just saying, "You're getting a 5 percent increase. That's all there is to it," is not a businesslike, professional statement. The complete requirements for an effective merit increase discussion are as follows:

• *Be precise.* Explain your company's salary policy clearly and concisely. Make sure you let employees know their present salary grade and the salary range. Let the employee know the amount and effective date of the increase.

• *Review the performance data upon which the salary decision was made.* If employees have concerns over the salary decision, don't argue with them. Respond openly and with empathy. Provide as much objective data as you can about the issues raised by each employee. The only "off limits" area of discussion should be the salary of other employees.

• *Make sure employees understand that the increase corresponds to their overall performance rating.* For example, a rating of "Usually exceeds requirements" for a person in the second quartile would normally result in an increase within the guidelines for that category. Try to carefully explain the rationale behind the amount of the increase.

• *Do not negotiate salary.* If you've done a good job of explaining the salary policy and have fairly evaluated the employee's performance, there's no need for you to feel defensive or apologetic. Don't blame "them," or "the system," or "the boss." Take ownership of the salary decision.

If the employee is unhappy with the increase, you should discuss how the person can increase her contributions to the organization, which could increase the likelihood of a larger increase in the future. Be careful not to make any promises you won't be able to keep. Remember the unknowns you're dealing with. The next performance review rating will be affected by the performance of others in the department and the amount of the merit budget will be affected by the salary plans of other companies as well as the financial performance of your own company. Be careful. You don't want irate people telling you later, "You promised me . . . ."

If you feel someone is being unfairly compensated, discuss this with your manager and human resources. Do this long before salary increase time. I can guarantee if you march down to human resources because your people have complained that their annual salary increases were inadequate, you'll get a defensive reaction from human resources. Instead, begin to work the issue months in advance. Human resources, hopefully, conducts an annual salary survey and can tell you if the person is competitively paid based on what others make both inside and outside your company. If an equity adjustment in base salary isn't appropriate, there might be other aspects of total compensation that can be examined—for example, a one-time bonus, stock options, or an increased salary incentive program. If HR indicates the person is fairly paid, you then have to buckle up and tell the person that research indicates his compensation is at an appropriate level. That's usually called "taking ownership," and that's what managers have to do.

Development Planning

Development planning is often dreaded by employees. Like the performance review, this process too often is a chance for a manager to "beat up" on an employee. People are told, "In order to be more well rounded you need to do . . . ." Frankly, the only people who need to be well rounded are cartoon characters. We tend to want to produce people who are "jacks of all trades and masters of none." People become successful not because they are well rounded or have an absence of weaknesses. They become successful because they have an expertise in something. That something should be based on what they love doing and have a passion for, and it must meet the needs of the organization. For too many managers, the only consideration is the needs of the organization. A more useful development plan is one where the manager asks questions rather than dictates development activities. Simple, straightforward questions such as:

- What do you want to become better at, either to improve current performance or prepare for greater responsibility?
- What kinds of activities would help you do that?

If employees aren't sure of what they want to do, that's fine. There should be a plan to help determine that. They could do information interviewing with members of management or other employees. They could shadow people on the job. They could work on a developmental assignment in a different department. They may learn that they like or don't like something. Either way, that's good to know.

Be careful not to talk to people about things they don't want to and don't have to do. For example, an individual development plan sounds like a good idea. But the way it's often implemented is a turn-off for many people. The manager may use it like a performance review—as a weapon to discuss someone's "weaknesses." Often, people are given lists of things they need to "do better" whether they want to or not. Instead, I'd recommend building on someone's strengths and interests. Typically the stronger people are in their area of specialty, the weaker they are in other things. In other words, someone who is a world-class pianist probably hasn't taken the time to learn to drive, to go out on dates, or to develop a taste for fine wines. Build on people's strengths. Don't dwell on their weaknesses. Talk to the world-class pianist about what interests him—playing the piano—and not about things he doesn't care about.

Here's how ridiculous many development discussions are. Let's say you were having one with Bill Gates. Imagine if it went like this:

> "Hi, Bill. It's time for our annual development discussion. You've concentrated on being a CEO and now you're going to be working full time on running your charitable organization. That's all well and good, but it's my job to point out the things you don't do well. So, I've written up a few of them. You don't know how to do needlepoint, so I've arranged for a class on it for you. Furthermore, you don't speak Swahili, so I suggest you take an online course to learn that language. I've also seen, in examining your records, that you aren't very good at curling. So, I'm going to ask you to join our company curling team. Okay, Bill. That's it for this time around. See you next year."

Maybe, unlike most employees, Bill dares to question management. He says, "But I'm not interested in any of those things. I don't want to do them." You'd say, "Look, Bill. I know what's best for you. I *strongly* suggest you follow my suggestions. You don't want to be accused of having a bad attitude, do you?" So, Bill leaves your office feeling defeated and discouraged. You check off the box that you've had another development discussion.

For those of you who have been around organizations for a while, you know what I'm talking about isn't that far removed from reality. I can remember the first development discussion I ever had with a boss. The VP of human resources (although not the same one I mentioned before) tried to talk to all the HR directors and managers in a single day. I had prepared what I thought were some good ideas of how I could do more of the things I wanted to do, especially since there were certain things I deeply cared about. Well, the meeting was scheduled for the morning and I finally got in to see him at 5:30 P.M. Naturally, he was "running late." I felt frustrated and angry even before the meeting started. He began by saying, "As you know, this has been a busy day for me. So, I'll cut to the chase and give you my master plan. What I want to do is swap some of the domestic directors with those overseas. Your next assignment will likely be in Europe. To help you prepare for that . . . ." He asked me no questions. Not even a "What do you think?" He never asked me what I wanted. I felt like a piece of furniture that could be moved on a whim. That was the day I knew my tenure with that company was going to be a short one. That was the one and only development discussion I ever had. You know, I don't feel badly about that at all.

Using the five-factor performance review system, Figure 9-3 shows the performance management and development issues managers should discuss with employees.

Figure 9-3. Performance and development issues.

Rating	Performance Issues	Development Issues
Far Exceeds	What higher-level responsibility can this person take on? Can the employee lead projects, teach others, and take over some of your duties?	In what development activities can this person participate to prepare for advancement?
Exceeds	How can this person improve performance to increase likelihood of a "Far Exceeds" rating?	In what development activities can this person participate to prepare for advancement or improve current performance?
Meets	How can this person improve performance to increase likelihood of an "Exceeds" rating?	In what development activities can this person participate to improve current performance?
Usually Meets	How can this person improve performance to increase likelihood of a "Meets" rating?	In what development activities can this person participate to improve current performance?
Below Requirements	How can this person improve performance to increase likelihood of a "Usually Meets" rating?	In what development activities can this person participate to improve current performance by a specified date?

Introducing Change:
From "Woe!" to "Wow!"

Conventional wisdom is that people resist change. That's not quite true. People resist *being* changed. We don't like to be forced to do things without an explanation. That's the way it happens too often at work. Information is essential to employees during change. They need to know exactly what needs to be done, how it needs to be done, and why it needs to be done. Many people feel uncertain and insecure during times of change. Most managers don't do a good job of providing information when things are in a normal state, let alone during times of significant change.

I have known people, as I'm sure you have, to go through the shock of change and be traumatized for a substantial period of time. I've known laid-off people who continue to "go to work" but sit in their car in the parking lot all day. I've known people who, after a major reorganization, stand in front of their closet, unable to choose what to wear to work, or stand in the cafeteria line, unable to choose what to have for lunch. I've known people to forget how to get to work, even if they've worked in the same building for years. They wind up on a strange road and don't know how they've gotten there. I've known experienced programmers to "get stuck" in the middle of a line of code and not remember how to program in a language they've used for years. Change can affect people in many ways. It can cause a sudden increase in divorce rates or alcohol and drug use; it can cause a spike in traffic accidents because people have trouble focusing. We're talking about dangerous stuff. Most managers don't even consider the serious effects of change on people, especially if the change is mishandled. Instead, they complain about employees' "resistance to change."

Stages of Transition Through Change

People transition through the change process in a predictable way. Almost everybody in almost every situation goes through the same basic stages. Some theorists have put forth a five-stage system; some talk about six stages, some seven. I like to think of it in simple terms and say there are four basic stages in the change process. The U-shaped arrow shown in Figure 10-1 represents energy. It can take days, weeks, months, or years to go all the way from the first stage to the final stage. Furthermore, there's no guarantee that someone will go all the way from the first to the final stage. It's very possible that someone could get stuck in a stage and stay there. It's unlikely that someone can skip stages. It's very rare that someone

Figure 10-1. Four stages of the change process.

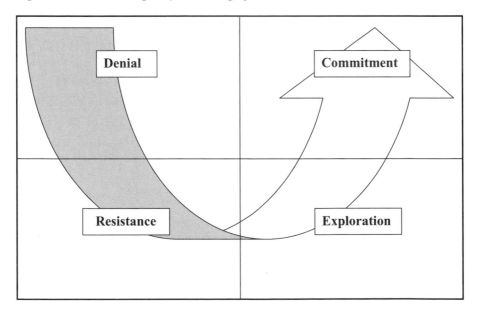

fails to go through these stages in the exact order presented. Change is like a traumatic event. It's easy to say "Just get over it!" but some people can't. It can stay with them a lifetime. The manager's job is not to prevent change. It's to get people to progress through the stages and get to the final one—commitment—as soon as possible. The stages are:

1. *Denial.* The immediate impact of the change is usually numbness. Someone doesn't know what to think. The safest thing to do, then, is to take a "wait and see" approach. "We'll cross that bridge when we come to it," or "You don't really believe that stuff, do you?" are common responses to major changes. A woman whose husband dies after fifty years of marriage might continue to wash his clothes, for example, and hang them in the closet. She's confused and really can't handle the change. "I just wish everyone would stop telling me what to do, she says, "I'll deal with this when I'm ready."

2. *Resistance.* There are two types of resistance—active and passive. Active resistance is when someone openly rebels against the change. It's easier for a manager to deal with active resistance because people come and tell you what they think. Passive resistance is much more common. It's when someone pays you lip service but withdraws their energy and enthusiasm. They might sabotage something by "forgetting" about it or "not having enough time" to do it. The newly widowed woman might "forget" about the appointment with the lawyer to discuss the execution of her husband's will. Or she "agrees" to fill out the insurance claim form but conveniently "loses" it. The focus during this stage is inward—people feeling sorry for themselves.

3. *Exploration.* Most healthy people after a suitable period of time will progress to the exploration stage, which involves thinking about and planning for the future. All of a sudden, the widow takes her husband's clothes from the closet and is ready to donate them to charity. One day she begins to talk about what she's going to do with the insurance money. Relatives might say, "We've been telling you this for months. It's about time." The truth is, she's ready now. She wasn't before. Now she has the mental and physical energy to look to the future.

4. *Commitment.* It's conceivable, but remember, not a given, that someone can go to the final stage. This is when they've embraced the

change, wrestled with it, examined possibilities, and now they're ready to move on. It's conceivable that they can be just as energetic and enthusiastic as they were before. In a company that has had a layoff, for instance, it may be a year or more before people get to this stage. You know that the widow in the example has gotten to the final stage when she's doing things she wasn't doing before—maybe buying new clothes, or joining a book club, or wanting to travel with friends.

"Supporting" Employee Movement Through the Stages

When information is poor, employees are more likely to feel anxious and insecure. They'll have trouble progressing through the stages. People who hear nothing usually fear the worst. What they dream up in the way of rumors is usually significantly worse than the truth of the situation. What can managers do to help? It can be summarized with the acronym SUP-PORTING:

Seeing other people's point of view

Unrestricted access to information

Positive thinking and optimism

Presence and proximity

Openness to the effects of the change

Rumors and gossip openly discussed

Thanking people for their cooperation and flexibility

Involvement

No change in values

Guidance

When I talk about the importance of "presence and proximity," it is because many managers make the mistake of disappearing during times of change or spend their days huddled with other managers behind closed doors. Involvement means that the more you share information and use people's ideas, the better they'll adapt to the change. (Think of it as "the more input, the more output.") You can also help employees by showing "no change in values," which means you should believe in the same things and stand for the same things in good times or bad. Finally, it's perfectly okay for you to say things like, "Here's what I think, " or "Here's my take on things," or "Here's the way I look at it." Many managers are afraid to give any guidance for fear that they'll be wrong. Sharing your personal opinion is always appropriate, even if you turn out to be wrong. People will still appreciate it.

When managers introduce change to the work group, they need to be thoroughly prepared with detailed background information. Time invested in gathering information will save considerable time and anguish in the future. If *your* manager doesn't know the reasons for the change and the impact it will have in your work group, find out who does. Get the information you need from that person. It is much easier and more efficient to take an approach that will *prevent* resistance before a change takes place rather than having to deal with resistance that has been built up *after* the change.

Explain completely how the change will affect your employees because this information will be their primary area of concern. The atmosphere of openness you create by asking for, and accepting, their reactions will help make them more receptive to the change. In fact, if the initial reaction is positive, ask them if they see any negative aspects of the change. Conversely, if the initial reaction is negative, ask for positive aspects. Do *not* avoid discussion of the unfavorable effects. The employees will experience them sooner or later, and if the employees bring these unfavorable effects to your attention later, they are more likely to voice them in anger as complaints.

By dealing with employee concerns openly, you will do much to alleviate their anxieties and reduce the threat of the change. Be sure to involve them as much as possible in all aspects of the change. Ask for employee ideas and use them, if at all possible. If a change is nonnegotiable, let your people know that. Tell them, "We need to implement this new policy and I need your ideas on how to make it work."

You may find certain employees will just not agree with the need for change. If this occurs, your task is not to argue or become defensive, but to accept the fact there may be an honest difference of opinion. Even though not everyone agrees with the change, don't be afraid to ask for a commitment to making the change successful. If you've done a good job in earning respect and credibility, you will likely have the loyalty of your employees. This, then, is a time when it may be appropriate for you to say things such as, "Could you do me a favor?" and "I'd appreciate your doing this for me."

The Winds of Change

Some changes you think will produce major upset go very smoothly. Other changes that you think will go very smoothly will produce major upset. The worksheets provided here are assessment tools that can help you plan for change. Pick an upcoming change happening in your organization and circle the appropriate point on the continuum for each of the ten factors. Then, see where it falls on the scoring analysis. Finally, go through each of the factors and look for how you can increase the odds of success for the change in the Action Plan.

"The Winds of Change" Assessment

While sunny weather makes us feel good, bad weather can unsettle and even frighten us. Let's take a look at how a change might affect organizational climate over a long period of time. Here are ten change factors to rate on a five-point scale. The ratings "1" and "5" are "highly descriptive" of the respective views. A "2" and a "4" are "moderately descriptive." A rating of "3" means "neither view is descriptive."

1. Relative Advantage: How is the change perceived?

1	2	3	4	5
People believe that it will help achieve something important that they want.			People do not see how the change will benefit them in any way.	

2. Impact on Social Relations: How will the change affect significant relationships?

1	2	3	4	5
Relationships will improve or remain positive.			Relationships will be harmed or remain negative.	

3. Scope of the Change: How much of the organization will be directly affected?

1	2	3	4	5

Implementation will affect only a few work areas.

Implementation will affect the entire company.

4. Complexity: How cumbersome is the change for people?

1	2	3	4	5

The change isn't difficult to understand or implement.

The change is extremely difficult to understand and implement.

5. Compatibility: How close does the change come to fitting with the existing culture?

1	2	3	4	5

The change represents values and beliefs that are the same as most people's.

The change represents values and beliefs that are the opposite of most people's.

6. Communication: How easy is it to let people know details about the change?

1	2	3	4	5

Communication has been excellent. The reasons for the change and steps to follow for success are widely known.

Miscommunication has already taken place. The reasons for the change and steps to follow for success are not widely known.

7. Timing: How much time will elapse between people being made aware of the change and when it actually will occur?

1	2	3	4	5

There will be sufficient time for planning, training, and full discussion of the nuances of the change.

Little, if any, time exists for planning, training, and full discussion of the nuances of the change.

8. Experience with This Type of Change:
How has the organization and/or the industry fared with similar changes?

1	2	3	4	5

Changes of this type have almost always met with success. The track record gives people confidence they can do it again.

Changes of this type have seldom met with success. Confidence is lacking because the track record is poor.

9. Amount of Involvement: How much ownership and commitment do people feel?

1	2	3	4	5

There has been widespread involvement in planning for this change so that most people feel the change is "theirs."

Very few people have been involved in planning for this change so that most feel the change is being forced on them.

10. Reversibility: How permanent are the effects of the change?

1	2	3	4	5

It will be relatively easy to reverse the change if things don't work out.

It will be impossible to reverse the change if things don't work out.

Scoring Analysis

How strong are the winds of change? Add the total number of points to get your organizational forecast.

Hurricane Force (44–50)—Extreme danger exists. Violent winds are producing raging tides; local tornadoes are probable. People will be on alert in case they have to evacuate. Awesome destructive power will be unleashed, producing loss of life and costing substantial amounts of money. Monsoon-like rains are predicted to drench inhabitants, producing an extreme chilling effect on morale and productivity. Local squalls are almost guaranteed to produce cold fronts, extreme pressure, and jockeying for power. It's going to be a fight for survival!

Tropical Storm (37–43)—Much danger exists. Intense winds are producing turbulent tides and breeding local tornadoes. Significant destructive power could be unleashed, producing loss of life and costing substantial amounts of money. Very heavy rains are predicted to drench inhabitants, producing a real chilling effect on morale and productivity. Local squalls will probably produce cold fronts, extreme pressure, and jockeying for power. Many people may have to fight for survival!

Tropical Depression (30–36)—Don't underestimate the danger that exists. There's a reason it's called "depression." Strong winds could produce very high tides and breed local tornadoes. Destructive power could be unleashed that may lead to loss of life and cost a great deal of money. Heavy rains are predicted to soak inhabitants and possibly produce a chilling effect on morale and productivity. Local squalls are likely to produce cold fronts, high pressure, and jockeying for power. Some people might have to fight for survival.

Gale Force (23–29)—Some danger exists. Strong winds could produce high tides and even cause local whirlwinds. It's unlikely there will be much evacuation. Destruction could lead to personal injury and cost some money. Heavy rains are predicted to wet inhabitants and possibly produce a chilling effect on morale and productivity. Local squalls might produce cold fronts, some high pressure, and jockeying for power. It's unlikely anyone will have to fight for survival.

Stormy Weather (16–22)—Little danger exists. Winds could produce tides higher than is typical, but local whirlwinds are not predicted. There is the possibility, however, of personal injury and loss of money if normal precautions are not taken. Rain can produce a dampening effect on morale and productivity. A chance of cold fronts, higher pressure, and some blustering by the usual people.

Fair Weather (15 points or less)—What a beautiful situation! Clear sailing ahead. Expect gentle breezes, comfortable temperatures, and just a chance of clouds. Bask in the sunshine of likely success. People will be on a high due to warm fronts and relatively little pressure. Life is so easy! There's only one problem with this kind of weather—you know it's not going to last!

"The Winds of Change" Action Plan

Although you can't stop bad weather, you can take precautions to help ensure people's safety and minimize damage. Answer the following questions about the change situation you've described. For every "Yes," describe specifically what you can do or recommend be done.

1. Can you get people to see that the change will help achieve something important that they want?

_____

_____

2. Can you help relationships to improve or remain positive?

_____

_____

3. Can you have the change affect only a few work areas at a time?

_____

_____

4. Can you make the change less difficult to understand or implement?

_____

_____

5. Can you help the change represent values and beliefs that are the same as most people's?

_____

_____

6. Can you improve communication about the change and ensure that the reasons for the change and steps to follow for success are more widely known?

_____

_____

7. Can you ensure there will be sufficient time for planning, training, and full discussion of the nuances of the change?

_____

_____

8. Can you link this change to changes that have almost always met with success? Can that give people confidence that they can do it again?

_____

_____

9. Can you make sure there is widespread involvement in planning for this change so that most people feel the change is "theirs"?

_____

_____

10. Can you make it relatively easy to reverse the change if things don't work out?

_____

_____

Another good way to plan for a change is to use a "force field analysis." Any change involves opposing forces—the benefits of change versus the drawbacks of the change. List both using the form in Figure 10-2. You

Figure 10-2. "Force field analysis" for clarifying a plan for change.

Benefits of the Change	Drawbacks of the Change

List the benefits and drawbacks of a pending change, then answer the following two questions:

• How could you increase the benefits of the change?

_____

_____

_____

_____

• How could you reduce the drawbacks of the change?

_____

_____

_____

_____

can do this exercise on your own, or you can make it a group activity with those affected by the change or those whose support you will need.

Researchers Salvatore R. Maddi and Suzanne C. Kobasa (1984) found that those who were best able to handle stress had certain characteristics in common. They called it the "hardy response." These people had high degrees of:

- *Commitment.* Hardy people have a dedication that is steadfast. They don't discourage easily.
- *Challenge.* They see the glass as half full rather than half empty. They may even get a sense of accomplishment in successfully handling difficult situations.
- *Control.* They worry about what they can do and not about what other people should do.
- *Connection.* They have a strong support network of coworkers, friends, family, and others in their professional community. In talking to others, they realize that they're going through the same difficulties that others have gone through.

You may want to look for these traits when recruiting people if you're in a high-stress environment. You should also talk to your people about the importance of behaving this way during times of change.

Maintaining Your Sanity: Handling Performance Problems

A lot of people equate discipline with punishing or hurting someone. They equate it with the discipline they received as a child—getting yelled at and maybe spanked. A more appropriate, adult-like way to look at discipline is holding people accountable for what they agree they're going to do. It's as simple as that. Once they commit to do something, they should be expected to do it. For instance, if you were the admiral in charge of an aircraft carrier group cruising in the Persian Gulf, you'd have someone assigned to a midnight watch. You would expect that person to actually show up. If he didn't, you'd put that person in the brig and brought up on serious charges. There are people "not showing up" in organizations every day. What happens to them? Nothing! Absolutely nothing! The people in a department say, "Why doesn't management do something about it?" The assumption is: "Because management doesn't really care." The manager usually gives a feeble excuse such as, "I don't want to upset anyone," or "I'm afraid that I'd make matters worse." I guarantee you a real admiral wouldn't worry about that.

Be the manager who *does* care. Yes, you care about people. You do the things we've talked about in other chapters. You're supportive and understanding. But, you also shouldn't let anyone mess with you. You've got to be able to "throw someone in the brig" if the employees don't follow through and "bring them up on charges." Maybe lives aren't at stake like in the aircraft carrier example, but the life of your department is at stake. If you allow people to push you around, no one is going to respect you. It's like dealing with kids. If you say, "You can't go out and play with your friends until you've cleaned your room," you've got to mean it. You have to be prepared to follow through. If you don't, you won't have the respect of your kids and they won't have clean rooms.

Dealing with Causes, Not Symptoms

If managers would only ask "Why?" more than they do, life would be better for everyone. That way you'd be dealing with causes and not symptoms. I can't tell you how many managers, for instance, came into my office and said something like, "I want to fire this person who has a terrible absentee problem." I would ask the simple, obvious question: "Why does he have an absentee problem?" The typical manager would say, "I don't know. Why don't you talk to him?" Most of the time, by the way, in a situation like that, the employee would admit skipping work "because I can't stand my manager and I need a mental health day from time to time." Dig down and find out why people do what they do and why they feel the way they do. A woman in labor has a bad attitude. I can attest to that fact. But it's not the attitude that's the problem. It's funny how once the baby is born, there is a remarkable improvement in attitude. So, when someone has a bad attitude, isn't motivated, makes too many errors, or whatever the problem might be, it would help to find out what's causing the problem. Then, have them agree to a solution and hold them accountable for those actions. After getting the person to admit that a problem does indeed exist, then:

- As a first choice, have them come up with the possible solutions to the problem. People are much more likely to make their own ideas work.
- If they can't come up with possible solutions, give them a little time. Say, "Why don't you think about it overnight and we'll meet first thing tomorrow."
- If they still can't or won't give you solutions, then give them a list of possibilities and ask them which are the most practical.

- If they can't or won't choose anything from the list you've offered, give them a little time to "think about it overnight," then meet with them again the next day.
- As an absolute last resort, tell them what they should do. This is when your back is against the wall. Recognize it will be "your idea" and not "their idea," so it's likely they won't have much commitment.

Whatever ideas you and the person agree upon, be sure to write them down. The employee may become anxious and say, "Are you writing me up?" I've learned the best thing to say at that point is, "No, I'm writing it down. That way neither one of us will forget what we've agreed to." The connotation of "writing someone up" is that you're going to get rid of them and just need some documentation. The connotation of "writing it down" should be to approach things in a businesslike way, so it's an agreement that can be referred to later.

Imagine going to a doctor and saying, "Can you give me something for my headache?" An experienced doctor uses the headache as a symptom of a problem. If you've got a brain tumor, that's the real cause. Cure the brain tumor and the headache goes away. Almost all employee performance problems are symptoms. You've got to find the cause and then take corrective action.

Address performance problems early. It's much easier to say to someone, "I noticed something that I want to point out to you. It's not a big deal and will be easy for you to correct. I just want to mention it before it becomes a problem." Most people wouldn't react badly to that kind of comment. Contrast that with the manager who says, "I've had it with you. You've been a poor performer for the last twenty-three years and I'm sick of it." I don't know anyone who would react well to someone saying that. It's like a fire. It really helps if you have heat sensors and smoke detectors and you deal with something when it's just starting. It's easy to correct that way. If, like most managers, you ignore a situation until it's a huge nine-alarm blaze, you'll have a crisis on your hands. Too many managers are pyromaniacs creating their own crises caused by neglect.

Get employee agreement that they have to make a change in their behavior. You can ask them to send you an e-mail, to confirm that they will make the change. On something significant, remember, you'll want to know exactly *how* they're going to do it. Then schedule a follow-up date to review progress. Without a follow-up date, people are likely to assume that you weren't serious about the matter in the first place. If things go well and there's improvement, it gives you an opportunity to praise and thank employees for their efforts. If things don't go well, you once again get their commitment and speak in stronger terms about the need for the change. However, don't threaten people. Most of the time, they'll react very negatively. Even if you have a written action plan stating that "failure to meet the terms of this agreement will result in further disciplinary action, up to and including termination," you're still on the employee's side. You should tell everyone, "I certainly don't want disciplinary action to happen. I have every confidence that you'll be able to fulfill the terms of our agreement. I'll do everything possible to help you." Don't ever give employees the feeling that you're "out to get them."

Make sure you let employees know *why* something is a problem. For example, if they're continually late, don't just say, "It's against our policy" to be late. Instead, say, "You've missed the first part of our product strategy meeting three times in the last three weeks. I need your input in those meetings. You're in direct contact with our field people and you're expected to present their viewpoint at these meetings." If people understand the reason why you need them to change their behavior, they're much more likely to do it. Everyone everywhere belongs to Generation "Why." A key management responsibility is not just to let them know you want something, but to explain *why* you want it, too.

Giving Feedback

When you give feedback, make sure it's timely. Don't save it up. If you said to someone, "That was a good meeting you ran last February," the person would probably say, "What meeting?" You then reply, "I don't really remember. I just have a note here to mention it to you. I've been carrying the note around for about ten months." If you're going to compliment someone about a meeting, do it right away. Even positive feedback will backfire if it's not timely. Saying, "Nice job on that project," doesn't mean much if it's six years later.

Make sure your feedback is about behavior that can be changed. Frustration is increased when you remind people of shortcomings over which they have no control. It's like saying, "I think you're too short. Why don't you grow?" Also be sure to objectively describe observed behavior and results rather than evaluate the individual. If you avoid evaluation, you reduce the likelihood of a defensive reaction. That's why I stress that performance evaluations are best led by employees, as described in Chapter 9.

Don't give employees negative feedback when you're angry with them. You'll say things you don't mean and you'll say things you're sorry for afterward. Be professional, calm, and objective. Talk facts and don't exaggerate. Avoid words like "Always" or "Never" because they invite the other person to bring up the exceptions to prove you wrong. Instead, use more conservative phrases like "You have a tendency" or "A number of times" or "Often." That way it will be very difficult for them to bring up the exceptions to prove you wrong.

Don't try to make people into something they're not. It's like they're chess pieces. They're all different and they all have certain abilities. Don't try to make a knight into a rook. Don't try to make a pawn into a bishop. Respect employees for what they are. It is management's job to win the chess game, given the pieces it has. Learn to use the pieces better.

The best way to think of yourself is as a teacher. The employee is your disciple. The word *disciple* actually means learner. So, when you're applying discipline, you're operating in a teaching mode. Let employees know in no uncertain terms what they can do better and teach them how to do it better or have someone else teach them. Criticizing or punishing them is not teaching them anything, other than to dislike and maybe avoid the person doing the criticizing or punishing. It's good that you want to give someone some feedback, but don't say, "You're not a team player. I want you to work on that." They'll have no idea what you want them to do. A teacher wouldn't simply say to a student, "I want you to learn about differential equations." It's your job to teach them. The best managers are always the best teachers.

The Frankenstein Syndrome

There's a tale of Gothic horror that strikes fear in the hearts and minds of people everywhere. No, it isn't Mary Shelley's *Frankenstein*. It's the story of the manager-employee relationship that's created in far too many instances in today's workplace. Although published in 1818, *Frankenstein* is disturbingly similar to what often happens in modern organizational life. The story can help managers understand how they can take good, decent people and turn them into cynical, bitter employees. These employees become shells of the enthusiastic, positive people they were when they joined the company. It leads to the "Frankenstein syndrome," where managers create their own monsters. Just like in the book, it's the poor monster who gets the blame. But who created the monster? Isn't Dr. Frankenstein at least partly at fault?

Why does it happen? In interviews, managers often describe idyllic job situations that bear little relationship to reality. They don't describe the way things *are*. They describe the way they *wish* things were. The manager says, "This company recognizes people for their contributions and provides unlimited growth opportunity. In addition, I appreciate hard work, encourage innovation, and provide as much responsibility as people can handle." Applicants leave with stars in their eyes, telling the folks back home what a great boss and great company they are joining. The managers are delighted to have the "old" or malcontent employee leave the job and welcome the bright, enthusiastic, and positive newcomer.

So, a new employee is hired. The manager, however, is unavailable during much of the employee's first day of work (or any day thereafter). The new hire soon realizes that the job is mundane, repetitive, and lacking in any real responsibility. The employee becomes disillusioned and frustrated. The manager asks for ideas but never does anything with them. She says, "My door is always open," but doesn't listen to what the employee says. She offers to investigate the situation and get back to the employee, but never does.

In addition, the manager withholds information, telling the employee that certain situations are management confidential and that employees do not have a need to know. If the employee tries to approach the manager, the answer is always, "Now is not a good time. Wait for things to settle down." Ideas and suggestions are met with responses such as, "That's not the way we do things around here."

There are numerous other frustrating incidents, such as the manager saying that a project has to be completed "first thing tomorrow morning."

The employee works through most of the night to get it done. Then, it sits on the manager's desk untouched for weeks. The employee longs for the management style that the manager spoke of during the interview but never has practiced. It's just as the monster in *Frankenstein* said: "Everywhere I see bliss, from which I alone am irrevocably excluded. I was benevolent and good; misery made me a fiend."

The manager is offended and becomes defensive, accusing the employee of having the infamous bad attitude. There's a power struggle between the manager and the monster—I mean, employee. After being accused of having a bad attitude by the manager, the employee, of course, does indeed develop a *really* bad attitude, just as the monster did: "I will work at your destruction, nor finish until I desolate your heart, so that you shall curse the hour of your birth."

The employee manages to tough it out for a year, but the first performance review is a disaster. The manager discusses attitude, personality, and intentions. The employee doesn't understand why these topics are being brought up and wants to know when the manager will begin discussing job performance. The employee complains of not being treated as a professional. The manager feels she has hired the wrong person. The employee feels the manager is out to get him. The manager goes to human resources and, as has happened many times before, makes remarks about the ungrateful, disrespectful employee. Dr. Frankenstein sums it up, expressing the desire "to wreak a great and signal revenge on his cursed head."

The HR manager thinks, "Just another personality conflict. A transfer is out of the question because no one will accept an employee with a bad attitude. Our managers have more than enough people like that already."

This brings the matter full circle. The employee goes on job interviews, citing lack of recognition, growth, appreciation, or responsibility as his reasons for wanting to change jobs. He describes the current job in words similar to Frankenstein's monster: "a hell of intense tortures, such as no language can describe." His new boss promises what the employee is looking for and the employee is impressed. He goes home saying, "What a great company and great boss I'm joining."

The old manager goes through the motions and says she is sorry to see the employee leave and wishes him well. She breathes a sigh of relief, though, because there will not be any more problems with this employee.

Just as Dr. Frankenstein lamented: "I lived in daily fear, lest the monster whom I had created should perpetrate some new wickedness." Thus, the story ends with the manager again trying to locate the best person to fill the job and describing an idyllic job situation. . . . The parallel between the story of *Frankenstein* and the manager is certainly a cause for concern. In the world of management, you often get what you have created.

Outstanding managers mold and nurture the people they hire—their "creations"—the same way they would nurture a child. Rather than focusing on weaknesses, they build on people's strengths. The best managers are gifted in being able to structure jobs, projects, and organizations so that talents and strengths are fully utilized and the impact of weaknesses is minimal. They bring out the best in people.

Think of the kind of support a leader gives people in any field of human endeavor. The leader says, "I know you can do it," while the follower says, "I'm not good enough. I can't do it." The persistence of the leader can be convincing. All of the successful people I know can point to someone who believed in them. They say, "There was someone who wouldn't let me quit. They were there to pick me up when I fell down. Without them, I wouldn't have made it." I don't know of a single exception. Every successful person has had someone like that in his life.

You can be that person! What an exciting opportunity for you. Someday, someone can say about you, "I owe it all to you. You said that you knew I could do it. You said I was good enough. You were there to pick me up when I fell down. Thank you." As a manager, you can make that kind of difference in someone's life. Maybe even a *lot* of someones.

Action Items for Developing Your Ability to Drive Results Through Your Organization

Results Orientation—Focusing employee attention and effort on attaining outcomes of importance to the business.

•   Review the previous year's work with your department and determine whether or not key business results were accomplished and why. Discuss lessons learned from the past year.

•   Have your staff brainstorm the most viable tactics for reaching your goals; formalize those ideas in a department operations plan.

•   Detail the coming year's work that needs to be accomplished, looking for any obstacles that may prevent results from being accomplished. Develop contingency plans for overcoming those obstacles.

•   Devise a "road show" approach to communicate your department's strategies and goals to people in other departments. Seek input on objectives and tactics that might affect them.

•   List all the tasks the department performs and have the group prioritize them. Make sure the group understands that an "A" priority (critical importance) should never be sacrificed for the accomplishment of a "B" priority (medium importance) or a "C" priority (low importance).

• Have all employees present their performance versus goals to the department each quarter. Where a goal is not being met or is in danger of not being met, they should present a recovery plan.

• Ask your people what they need more of (or less of) from you to accomplish their goals for the year.

• Ensure that you give some form of positive recognition to someone each day.

• Be sure development activities are tracked just the same as normal work goals, and that people are recognized for their efforts in increasing their value to the organization.

• Create a record of the things that people in the department have done to develop themselves in the past, and be sure to share those ideas with newcomers.

• Rotate people through positions to give them a better understanding of the department's activities.

• Specify a plan to get your strongest performers promoted and, in turn, specify a plan to get your weakest performers up to speed.

• Get into the habit of sending people e-mails when you praise or criticize any aspect of their performance. It gives both activities more "bite."

• Let people talk about their feelings, not just report on projects and work goals, during one-on-one meetings and staff meetings. This is particularly important during times of stress or major changes.

• Seek out people if you think they are feeling stress. Vow never to be caught by surprise by having an employee resign and never to react by saying, "I had no idea this person was dissatisfied."

• Publicize department success stories in a blog or website. Be sure your management knows about these heroic activities.

• When there's a major change that will affect your department, seek out someone who has already led a group through the change and find out what worked and what didn't work.

• Be sure to hire and promote people who are at their best during times of change. Avoid the whiners and complainers, even if they are technically qualified.

•   Thank people before, during, and after they're involved in changes. Remember that people will tend to do what's rewarded and recognized.

•   Be sure to reward people with merit increases and performance review ratings commensurate with their contributions.

Lifelong Development

C H A P T E R   1 2

Career Planning

What does it take to get ahead? The typical response is that you have to "put in your time." But there are probably some things you should be doing while you're putting in your time. It's not that people are withholding information from you. It's probably that they don't know what you ought to be doing. The truth is, there's no "seeing eye" looking out for you, making sure you're treated fairly and getting the right opportunities. The only "eye" looking out for you sounds the same but is spelled differently—"I." You've got to take matters into your own hands. Decide on a goal and develop a plan outlining how you'll accomplish it. Put it in writing and change it as often as you need to. If you just "take it one day at a time," you'll likely feel frustrated about your career progress. Although luck can certainly play a part, it usually has little to do with realizing goals. You don't consistently accomplish your day-to-day work assignments, for example, by relying on "luck." Think of a career plan the same way. There's a big difference between sitting back and wishing for something to happen and focusing your efforts on implementing a well-formulated, thoroughly researched plan.

Steps to Follow

These steps may help you and those you coach in your organization:

• *Be specific.* Visualize the end-result and write a description of what you want to accomplish. Saying that "I want to be head of the internal audit department within five years" is a better goal than "I want a job where I'll feel challenged." Without a specific target, you'll have nothing to shoot for. You can change that target as many times as you want.

• *Challenge yourself.* Your goal should require you to do something that will allow you to grow and improve yourself. Goals are stimulating when you commit yourself to actions that will inspire you to go beyond what has been your best effort. For example, "I want to be a world-class expert in artificial intelligence" is an invigorating, exciting goal. Whether it happens or not isn't the point. It's the journey, the trying to get there, that makes life interesting.

• *Be realistic.* Keep in mind your current skills and abilities, your family situation, and other factors that are important to you. A good reality check is to talk to those who are now doing what you want to do. Ask them about the odds of success. Think of how many people also want to do what you want to do. How competitive are you compared to other people?

• *Pay the price.* After you have analyzed how realistic your goal is, decide how much you *really* want it. To achieve anything worthwhile, you have to sacrifice something. The more ambitious you are, the more you have to sacrifice. Many people talk about sacrificing, but they really don't mean it. Test your commitment. Decide how much energy, money, time, and other resources you're willing or able to commit. Imagine someone who wanted to become a world-class athlete but wasn't willing to invest the time in training. It just isn't going to happen.

• *Obtain appropriate knowledge and skills.* What will be required for you to successfully perform the position to which you aspire? How much of the requisite knowledge and skills do you have now? What's your plan to close the gap? This is where most people get lost. They formulate a goal but can't seem to figure out what to do to get there.

• *Break your goal into pieces.* As any dieter knows, saying, "I will lose two pounds this week" is a step on the way to saying, "I will lose forty pounds in the next six months." Draw a time line that illustrates when you will do key activities that will lead you to your eventual goal.

• *Determine what you can do right away.* It's essential that you get started. If not, your good intentions will amount to nothing. Your goal may be to "learn more about company systems." Your short-term action may be to "ask my manager, on Monday, if I can talk to Vincent about the XYZ system and act as a backup when he's on vacation or overloaded." Short-term actions will increase your confidence because you'll start to experience small successes. Step-by-step, you'll be working toward accomplishing your goal.

• *List potential roadblocks.* You've made some assumptions in formulating these plans. There is always some degree of uncertainty about the future. You may want to manufacture buggy whips and then suddenly someone invents the automobile. You may want to become an oil baron and then the world's supply of oil dries up. What are the obstacles or changes that could get in the way of your accomplishing your goal?

• *Develop contingency plans.* Assuming all of the things that could go wrong do, in fact, go wrong, what actions could you take to prevent your career plan from becoming derailed? In other words, have a Plan B, a Plan C, etc.

• *Ask "why?"* This is a crucial question. Before you charge off, ask yourself about your career goal. Listen carefully to the answer. Your reason should fit your interests, values, and needs. If it doesn't, you may be kidding yourself. If you say, "I want to become a senior vice president," but you fail to take into account the extra hours, stress, and pressure you'll have to endure, you may wind up an unhappy person.

• *Don't keep it a secret.* Career plans are only useful if they are shared. Let others, at home and at work, know how you have answered these questions. Get their advice and solicit their active support. They may be in a position now or in the future to help you. Vow not to ever have anyone say to you, "I'm sorry but I had no idea you were interested in that. I wish you had let me know." If that happens, guess what? It's too late.

Core Competencies

Every reader of this book may have a different career goal, but what everyone has in common is a need to develop certain competencies. A competency is a behavior that top performers are likely to utilize more often and more completely for better results. Are there certain qualities or characteristics that successful people have? Having tracked thousands of people through organizations, I would propose to you that there are some qualities that lead to success in virtually every profession. Even if you have no idea whatsoever of what you want to do in the future, you would do well to pay attention to these dozen competencies:

- Analytical Thinking
- Business Understanding
- Confidence
- Developing Self
- Effective Communication
- High Standards
- Initiative
- Persistence
- Responsiveness to Customers
- Teamwork
- Thoroughness
- Technical Skills

There are a number of ways to begin to get a handle on your relative strengths and weaknesses. For example, you could do a forced ranking of how effective you are in each area by rating the competencies—for example, "1" for your strongest competency to "12" for your weakest. Then, you could have other people rate you as well. Or you could take each competency and rate it a "1" for "outstanding" or a "5" for "poor," or some number in between. Again, you could have others rate you as well. Make an assessment of your core competencies a part of your plan and get started using the insight you've gained. Don't wait for things to come to you. If you're a dairy farmer, for example, it's best to go out and get the cows. You could wait for them to come to you, but I don't think you'll get as much milk that way. Once in a while, one will wander over to you, but I'm going to put my money on the farmer who goes out and gets what he wants.

Core Competency Action Items

Here are some ideas to stimulate your thinking as you put together your career plan.

1. *Analytical Thinking.* You must be able to analyze situations to identify patterns, explanations, and causes of problems.

- When you're confronted with a complex issue, think about whether you have dealt with similar situations in the past. If so, what was similar? What was different? What worked well in the previous situation that would work with your current issue? What didn't work, and what can you do to prevent similar problems from occurring in your current situation?

- If a project, issue, or situation doesn't make sense to you, ask questions that will help you gain a greater understanding. Doing so may also help others to think of other useful questions. Ask the key information-gathering questions: who, what, where, when, why, and how.

- Before taking a particular action as a solution to a problem, ask yourself if you have identified the *real* problem and therefore the *best* solution. For example, if the printer isn't working, is a service call really required or is it just out of ink? You can solve many problems yourself simply by stepping back and looking at the situation from different perspectives.

- Learn about problem-solving and decision-making tools such as "pros and cons," "costs versus benefits," and "return on investment." Use them to help analyze situations and determine the best course of action.

- Take advantage of the "extra mileage" you can get out of the work you are doing for one project or assignment to help enhance the other.

- Ask your manager or others around you to suggest problem-solving processes or resources rather than simply giving you the answers or solutions you seek.

- Ask peers to review your work plans or time lines to reality-test them for orderliness, assumptions, and dependencies. Revise your plans to reflect any recommended changes that make sense. Double-check key project details periodically to ensure completeness and accuracy.

• Identify people who excel at logical problem analysis, project planning, or work organization. Ask them to describe their thinking and planning processes to you. Learn from their experiences. Apply the best practices to your own work.

• Before developing a solution from scratch to a seemingly new problem, review previous projects. Rather than reinvent the wheel, identify existing solutions that are appropriate enough to adapt.

• Review recently completed projects as a way to improve future planning. Identify and make note of predictable obstacles and dependencies that can affect schedules and outcomes.

• When faced with a complex problem or project, identify different viable solutions/approaches by seeking out multiple sources. Get input and suggestions from your manager as well as peers. Remember to get input from those in other parts of the organization whose areas will be affected.

• Use project planning software and planning methodologies to break down your projects more systematically and identify critical path items, benchmarks, and key deliverables.

2. *Business Understanding.* You must develop and demonstrate an understanding of the business and the way things get done in the organization.

• Request copies of organization charts and study them. Do you understand the importance of each job on the chart and how it relates to others? Ask if you need clarification on the purpose of any of the jobs and functions.

• Develop a work flowchart (i.e., a map of how work flows to you, from you to the next person, from that person to someone else, and so on). Make it a goal to understand who and what is involved in a project or task before you become involved. Find out what happens with work once you are done with your piece.

• Attend staff meetings of other departments and invite others to *your* staff meetings to talk about their functions.

• Regularly read your company's marketing literature, website information, recent press releases, and financial disclosures.

- Attend the annual stockholders meeting and read the minutes or analyst briefings and stock recommendations.

- Develop a vision statement on what you do, how that contributes to the work of your department, and how you and your department contribute to company success.

- Ask your manager for assignments that require you to be a member of cross-functional work teams. Use these opportunities to find out about the responsibilities of others.

- Attend company-sponsored training programs and network with other participants.

- Have a goal of meeting and getting to know at least one person in every department of your company.

- See if you can get a development assignment that would temporarily put you in another function. For example, if you're a field person, work in the home office; if you're a staff person, work in a line function; if you're a corporate person, work in a division.

- Initiate one-day job swaps or job shadowing with peers in other departments or work groups to build an understanding of how other people's jobs fit into your company.

- Ask your manager to spend some time during each staff meeting providing your work group with information on company business plans, objectives, products, and services. If your manager isn't well versed in these issues, invite people who are.

- After receiving business updates at staff meetings, think about how any changes affect your own work and goals. Do you need to adjust? Develop new or revise existing processes or systems? Reprioritize projects or activities?

- Before beginning each new assignment or project, ask yourself, "What business objective will I be contributing to or accomplishing?" If you can't answer this question, ask for more information in order to develop a better understanding of the overall business context for your work.

- Attend a new employee orientation, obtain any DVDs of trade show presentations, and read the marketing literature used to promote the company's business. In particular, look for product or business strategies that might alter the company's future landscape.

3. *Confidence.* You must demonstrate belief in yourself and your capabilities by taking needed action in complex, unclear, problematic, or risky situations.

• Identify your strengths and find ways to use them to contribute to your department or help others.

• Concentrate on maintaining eye contact with people when you speak with them face-to-face. Practice with friends in casual conversation as a way of getting used to making eye contact in other situations.

• Develop comfort and confidence in presenting your point of view by practicing what you say and how you say it with peers. Ask them for feedback and make use of any helpful input.

• Avoid using self-defeating language. Work at replacing such statements as "This probably doesn't make sense but . . ." with more positive, self-confident phrases like, "I've got a quick and easy way to get the results we need."

• Identify an aspect of your job (e.g., computer skills, customer interactions, or conducting meetings) where you could improve. Focus on developing your skills in this area as a way to build confidence in your overall capabilities.

• When faced with a particularly difficult or complex problem, don't isolate yourself to work it out. It can be useful to seek the help and input of others. Talk through the situation with your manager or a peer.

• Ask others for their ideas and listen with an open mind. This shows that you are confident enough to consider all the options before making up your mind.

• Manage your saturation point. Don't seek input to the point where you are overwhelmed with choices or ideas. Instead, identify a couple of people who can provide you with the most valuable advice and then take some time to sort through what you've heard.

• Look for opportunities to make stand-up presentations. Nothing builds self-confidence more than a successful presentation to top management or to customers. Work first with subject matter, and with groups, where you are most comfortable. Then expand the audience and the range of topics.

• Practice engaging in conversations with others you do not know well. Introduce yourself. Explain your background and work on posture, presence, and the way you present yourself.

• Remind your manager and others who have input into your performance review that it is important for you to know when you are working effectively, as well as when you need improvement. Positive reinforcement of successful performance builds self-esteem.

• Look for opportunities to work on projects or technologies that have a moderate degree of challenge associated with them. The danger of working exclusively in areas where you are already proficient is that your perception of your ability to work outside your comfort zone can diminish over time.

• Talk through your thinking with your manager as a way of developing the manager's confidence in your ability to handle challenging issues or projects. Even if your manager is confident in your ability to handle complex situations, meet with him to mutually agree on the kinds of assignments you can take on with minimal guidance.

4. *Developing Self.* This competency is about seeking and taking advantage of opportunities to strengthen your current skills and develop new ones.

• Find instructor-led or online courses that seem interesting and useful to you, then ask your manager if you can sign up. The Internet has a plethora of courses listed on websites such as www.SeminarInformation.com and www.TrainSeek.com. If you simply used "Training" as a search word, you'd find tens of thousands of listings.

• See what courses your company offers in-house. In addition to getting concepts and ideas from the training, you'll have the opportunity to get away from work for a day and think about the way you do things and how you can do them better. This is much more useful than a "mental health" personal day off.

• When you meet someone else in the company whose work sounds interesting, ask if you can spend a half-hour or a lunch break with them to learn about what they do and what skills are required to do their job. If you think you'd like to work in this area in the future, plan ways to develop the required skills.

• Identify job responsibilities or activities with which you are uncomfortable. Determine whether your discomfort is due to a need for additional skills or expertise. If so, identify what additional knowledge you need and make plans to obtain it.

• When you complete an assignment, assess your work. What worked well and what was difficult? Present your thoughts to your manager and ask where she agrees or disagrees with your assessment. Identify steps you can take to minimize difficulties on future assignments.

• Identify someone from your own or another work group who is really good at something you need to learn or do better. Ask if you can assist that person on an assignment so that you can learn by observing.

• Ask for coaching and developmental direction from managers or peers who have capabilities you need in order to do your job better or to be more productive.

• Ask your internal/external customers for a detailed assessment of your performance—what you do well and areas that you need to develop. Write out a plan that focuses on improving in one of those areas. Make sure to articulate specific measurements of success, and try to set checkpoints when you will review your progress with your customers to make any necessary adjustments.

• Identify people in your own or other work groups who are recognized as star performers in areas where you'd like to improve.

Ask them how they developed in those key areas (e.g., what courses they took, what on-the-job or off-the-job activities helped them, what assistance they received from their managers) and translate any relevant ideas into development plans for you.

• Ask your manager to keep you informed about volunteer or special projects with which you can get involved. Focus on activities that will provide you with skills you don't currently have but could use in your present job.

• Learn how to use relevant technologies, tools, or systems that your peers in other work groups are already using to get their work done more efficiently.

• Complete your degree or audit college courses. Explore online learning from sources such as the University of Phoenix (www.universityofphoenix.com). Most universities now offer accredited courses with little or no residency requirements.

• After an interaction with your manager, customers, or peers, think about what went well and what could have been better. Plan ways to improve your process, skills, or results before the next interaction.

5. *Effective Communication.* You must communicate information so that it makes an impact, is easily understood, and is useful to others.

• Meet with your manager to assess your communication skills and identify developmental needs. Ask for recommendations in terms of specific training programs or other specific actions you can take to become a more effective communicator. Go to presentations made by members of top management, sales and marketing people, or others who are expert communicators. Analyze what they say and how they say it.

• Listen when someone is speaking to you and demonstrate that you understand by summarizing and repeating back to them what they have said to you and the significance of it. Effective communication isn't just about being an expert at talking. It's about being an expert at listening, too.

• When writing:

- "Speak" on paper (i.e., think of how you would say something to a friend and then write it that way).
- Find ways to simplify the information you need to communicate. Use bullets, charts, and diagrams.
- Use simple, straightforward language that everyone can understand.

• Watch for communication habits that cause others to react positively or negatively and learn from this assessment what you can do better or differently.

• Ask another person to critique your use of different modes of communication and make suggestions for how you can use each more effectively. Focus on one form of communication (e.g., e-mail, telephone, face-to-face, videoconferencing) at a time.

• Ask a peer to observe you over the course of a week and note your communication strengths and "bad habits." (Do you interrupt people in midsentence? Do you ramble on a voice mail because you haven't prepared your message ahead of time? Do you look away when people are talking to you? Are your e-mails unclear, and do they have typos?) Afterward, identify action steps and a time line for capitalizing on your strengths and kicking your bad habits. Check your progress regularly with your peer.

• Reserve time at the end of each week to review all of the critical actions you took that week. Did you pass on information about any actions, decisions, or plans to the people who will be affected or have a need to know? If not, make it a priority to communicate better next week.

• Before preparing any communication, consider the makeup of your audience. For example, will you be conveying technical information to someone who isn't technical? Identify a format to use that is clearest and most useful for your audience.

• Prepare your communications as if you will be questioned or challenged on the material you are providing. Have backup data ready in case it is needed.

• Pair up with someone in your work group whose communication you can review for accuracy and effectiveness and who can, in turn, do the same for you. You'll learn as much from critiquing someone else's work as you will from having *your* work critiqued.

•   Identify files, templates, menus, manuals, or other documentation that you and others use on a regular basis that could be more clear, organized, or up-to-date. Take it upon yourself to revise or organize the material so that information is more easily accessible and useful for everyone.

6.   *High Standards.* You should be setting and maintaining work standards that demand excellent performance.

•   Find out exactly what is expected of you and determine the steps you'll need to take in order to meet, and hopefully exceed, those expectations. Plan ahead to allow yourself enough time to get the critical work done properly. Don't let yourself become distracted by less important things.

•   Ask your manager for specific, concrete examples of what "outstanding" work looks like for your group, then identify what you need to do to bring your own performance up to or beyond what is expected.

•   When faced with the potential of having to compromise on quality, ask yourself what you would do if it were your own business and your personal reputation was on the line. Pursue that path of action.

•   Think about the saying, "If you don't have time to do it right, when will you have time to do it over?" Identify a time when you *did* have to do it over. Keep this in mind as you approach future tasks or projects.

•   Manage and meet your obligations. For example:

•   When you say you'll do something, do everything possible to meet that commitment.

•   If you owe someone an answer or a deliverable, let them know how you are progressing, even if you don't yet have what they need.

- Use checklists and a calendar to keep track of what you need to do.

- Anticipate potential obstacles to your plans. Determine steps you can take ahead of time to prevent them from slowing you down or stopping you.

• Learn about and use existing processes and procedures that have proved effective in ensuring the attainment of high performance standards in your department or work group. Don't ask the poor performers. Ask the superstars how they get it done.

• Set personal objectives that force you to aim higher and accomplish more than what's required for your job. That way, "falling short" of your goals means, at worst, accomplishing what was required.

• Treat all your tasks and assignments as works-in-progress, open for review by someone else at a later date, even after you've formally "closed the book" on the project. Doing your work with this mind-set will help you to constantly look at ways to enhance your results.

• Identify top-performing work groups in your company and other organizations and compare your work group to those benchmarks. What do those other groups do that make them "best in class"? Adopt their best practices to enhance the performance of your own team.

• Ask your peers to periodically critique your work. Be responsive to suggestions they have as to how you can raise your level of performance. In turn, ask your peers if you can make respectful, tactful suggestions to them.

• Look back over your work from the past year and identify a time when you chose the easiest rather than the best path of action. How was the result affected by your choice? Will you make a different choice if faced with a similar situation in the future?

7. *Initiative.* This competency is about taking action independently or before it is required by others or the situation.

- Look for opportunities or assignments to build your manager's confidence in you and your capabilities (e.g., offer to draft the budget or do the research needed in preparation for a task).

• Work with your manager to establish some operating guidelines that empower you to make decisions or take action independently (i.e., without your manager's prior review or approval) while ensuring you act in the best interests of the company and your department.

• When you see something that needs to be done, take the necessary steps to do it immediately. For example, if you go to use the copier and find out that it's jammed, don't just walk away. Clear the jam. Make a habit of taking immediate action rather than waiting for someone else to do it.

• Don't wait for deadlines to find out that something someone was working on for you isn't going to get done. Touch base with the person periodically before the deadline to find out how it's going. If the person is having trouble, help him to figure out how to solve the problem and still meet the deadline.

• When you have a suggestion or idea, don't wait to be asked about it. Identify an opportunity to voice your suggestion or idea and do so.

• Note when your manager or others in your work group could use your help and offer to take over a task or part of an assignment to relieve their burden. It's likely they'll help you in return when you need it.

• Look at future business events your manager has scheduled. Identify what may be required for the event and ask if you can go ahead and get started on what's needed well in advance.

• Ask your manager to be more "hands off" on projects once she has outlined the basic project requirements and to let you take responsibility for working out the details. Determine checkpoints in the project timeline when you and the manager can review your work together, to ensure you are accomplishing what's needed or to redirect your efforts, if necessary.

• Ask your manager and others in your department for feedback on your performance after you have completed a project in which you took a greater role or more responsibility than usual. Ask for specific examples of what you did that was effective. Ask for specific ways you could have been even more effective.

• Identify a recurring problem for your work group (e.g., work gets held up by one or two people at the end of the month when they become busy preparing reports) and take it on yourself to develop and implement a solution to the problem. Outline your plans with your manager and others in your group to get their input and buy-in before proceeding with implementation.

• Pick one important knowledge area in your department for which you can develop particular expertise or be the primary source of information. For example, you may be the best person for troubleshooting software problems or building process maps. Learn all you can to gain credibility, and let your manager and work group know you're willing to be a resource available to them.

• Take on tasks or assignments that require you to develop new skills. Make sure you target skills that are realistically within your capacity to develop. However, don't offer to develop a new computer program to replace the existing one if you aren't technically able to do it. Taking on unrealistic projects or assignments invariably will backfire and cause others to lose confidence in you.

• Before taking action or going ahead on projects of your own initiative, determine what the risk factors may be, and make sure you and others involved can live with them. For example, your manager agrees to let you implement a new process or procedure that you designed, with the condition that you get it up and running within thirty days. Do you have other obligations that you may not be able to meet, given this condition, and is that acceptable to everyone involved?

• Review solutions you have developed for specific problems or issues over the past six months. If appropriate, convert them into a core process or standard operating procedure to prevent or minimize recurring problems for your work group.

8. *Persistence*. This competency is about not giving up easily. You must continue to attempt to achieve results or obtain information until the desired goal is reached.

- If you think you can't do something, ask yourself *why*. Try to identify the skill, knowledge, or resources you lack that prevent you from being able to finish the job. Then seek a way to acquire what you need so that you *can* do it.

- Work with people who are known for being persistent and successful in pursuit of answers or resolutions to problems. Observe what they specifically do and adopt techniques that make sense for you.

- When you've asked other people to do something for you and they tell you it can't be done, ask them to explain what steps or action they've tried. Getting others to talk through their actions with you sometimes brings a new idea to mind that they hadn't thought to try.

- Remember to use all resources available to you. When you are having trouble accomplishing a task or assignment, ask for advice and suggestions from experts who have successfully completed similar assignments, both inside and outside your company.

- When you encounter resistance from someone whose help you need, put yourself in that person's shoes. Think of times when you were unable to help someone. What prevented you from helping someone else? What could the other person have done to get you to be more responsive? Use observations about your own resistance to guide you in getting others to be more cooperative and helpful.

- Acknowledge other people's persistence as a positive rather than negative behavior. This will make them more open to accepting persistent behavior from you.

- Try different ways of phrasing requests or questions when your initial attempt doesn't work. It may simply be a lack of understanding rather than an unwillingness to cooperate that prevents others from being helpful to you.

• When you are having particular difficulty getting the desired response from someone in your own or another department, seek advice from someone who interacts with that person on a regular basis to learn what approach they've found to be successful.

• Ask others how they "get to yes" or finally achieve success, even after encountering significant obstacles. Try out techniques or approaches that make sense for the situation you're in. Make note of what works and what to do differently next time.

• Try to anticipate when you will encounter resistance or difficulty, then plan a course of action in advance. In your plan, include alternative routes you can take so that you don't get permanently sidetracked or blocked from succeeding.

• When talking with others who aren't doing what you need in order to move a task or assignment along to completion, think about what they will gain or how they will benefit from completing their part. Appeal to these benefits as a way of convincing them to take the necessary action.

• Learn to recognize "red flags" in things that people say or do, because they are signals that you are likely to encounter a problem. For example, someone may say, "Let me talk to my boss about it." What they probably mean is, "I don't want to do this job and I want to make sure my boss will back me up." Determine what steps or actions you can take to quickly determine if you're going to have a problem.

9. *Responsiveness to Customers.* Always make the needs of internal and/or external customers a priority when making decisions and taking actions.

• Before talking in-depth with customers, take time to review existing files, e-mails, and other documentation on them to understand any relevant background issues. This effort will help to prevent or minimize problems or misunderstandings on your part.

• Make sure you know who your customers are and what they need. For each customer:

- List what you think your customer needs.

- Check with the customer to see how accurate your list is.

- Make sure that you can meet the customer's needs. If you can't, negotiate with them on how to get their needs met.

- Reach a mutual understanding on what, specifically, you'll provide for your customer, then put it in writing and e-mail that information to the customer.

• Impress on customers the fact that you intend to meet their needs by asking them questions and by listening attentively to their requests. Aim to get the complete details by asking them how they plan to use what you provide to them, what the deadline is, and what else will help you to be more responsive to them.

• Practice refining your understanding of what customers are asking for by summarizing/restating their requests and asking them if you've understood them correctly.

• Think about a time when you received excellent service from a company or department. What made it so good? How can you do the same things for your customers?

• Spend some time on-site with customers so that you'll be able to see things from their perspective.

• Ask your peers what resources they use (e.g., contacts in other departments, computer programs, directories or manuals) that help them answer or provide accurate information to customers in an efficient manner.

• Ask questions to learn the context within which your customers work and within which their requests are formed. This effort will help you to better see issues from their perspectives and respond in a more empathetic way.

• Set response-time deadlines when you are working on a customer request or issue. Tell the customer when you will call back with a final resolution (e.g., by the end of the day). Customers will feel you're being attentive and haven't forgotten about them.

• Review work you're doing for customers periodically throughout the day to determine if any requests or issues that arise later in the day should take priority over any that came earlier in the day. Doing things on a "first come, first served" basis may not be the best approach for you. Ask for guidance if you're unsure about how to prioritize customer requests or issues.

• Use fifteen or twenty minutes at the end of each day to quickly review your work. Determine if there are any customer requests or issues that are unresolved. Take any additional action possible before you leave for the day to resolve issues that you can; otherwise, prepare to address the issues first thing the next day. For example, pull any necessary files and let customers know they're at the top of your "to do" list for the next day.

• Anticipate customer interactions that will be difficult for you. Ask your manager or peer to act the part of "the customer" and role-play the interaction with them. Try different approaches and ask for feedback and suggestions on how to handle the situation more effectively.

• Identify peers who are known for being responsive to customers and ask if you can listen or observe them as they interact with customers. Make note of what they say, how they say it, and what they do both before and after these interactions. Ask them to debrief you on what their thinking was behind the things they did. Identify the actions and techniques of these customer-oriented peers that you can use.

• Develop a system for regularly getting updates on changes that will affect your work. Don't wait until someone calls with a request or problem to discover requirements have changed.

10. *Teamwork*. Working cooperatively and respectfully with others within and across functions and at all levels of the organizations is a vital competency.

• Think about the saying, "Two heads are better than one," and identify a time when a project you worked on had a great outcome because of the involvement of a number of people. What contributions did the different team members make that helped the project turn out so successfully? Keep these thoughts in mind, and make sure to include others when planning future tasks or projects.

• Approach team decisions with an open mind. Working in a group usually means making the best decisions for the group, but not necessarily going with the decision you would personally choose.

• Treat disagreements you have with others not as conflicts but as opportunities to gain a better understanding of ideas that differ from your own and to clarify your own viewpoints.

• Seek feedback from your manager and peers on your effectiveness as a team player. Ask for and follow their specific suggestions for how you can be more collaborative.

• Always approach your work as if preparing it for someone you really want to impress.

• Before taking any action, build support for new ideas by seeking input from members of your team and including their most useful suggestions in your action plans.

• Interview managers and peers of successful teams to pick up tips that facilitate teamwork.

• Model teamwork by using staff meetings to facilitate the sharing of ideas, innovations, and best practices among your peers.

• Actively participate in meetings with other departments. Focus on developing or improving cooperation between departments in order to increase efficiency or effectiveness in handling mutual issues.

• Determine what prevents you from participating in team-oriented or collaborative projects or assignments. Are you, for example, self-conscious about your public speaking ability? If so, take action to build your self-confidence; practice and prepare yourself for participating in more public situations.

• Take a diversity workshop to improve your ability to see the unique and positive characteristics of team members whose backgrounds, education, and experience are different from your own.

- Volunteer to coordinate a social get-together for your work group so that team members will have the opportunity to develop a stronger business rapport by getting to know each other on a more personal level.

11. *Thoroughness*. Attend to the details to ensure that work is done correctly and completely.

- Take notes when you are assigned a task. As you work on the task, check your notes to be sure that your work is on target. When you have finished doing what you've been asked to do, double-check the actions you took against your notes to be sure you've left nothing out.

- When receiving a request from someone, ask questions:

    - Make sure you understand what you've been asked to do and how it contributes to what is needed. If the request doesn't make sense to you, it could be because you didn't hear the request the way it was intended.

    - Make sure you get all the necessary details by asking questions not only when you get the assignment but while you work to complete it.

    - Make sure you understand how your work affects the work of the person who has requested it of you. Asking questions will help ensure your work is on target.

- When someone gives you information upon which you'll base a decision or action, ask the person where the information came from and how she knows it is accurate.

- Before turning in completed work, double-check it for accuracy and completeness. Also ask a peer to review it. A fresh pair of eyes can often catch errors that familiar eyes overlook.

- Develop a method for tracking your work to ensure that you don't overlook any project tasks or steps. Your tracking method should also include steps for informing people when you have completed work they have requested of you.

• Swap jobs with peers in other work groups that you interact with on a regular basis in order to fully understand how what you do contributes to or affects other departments or work groups.

• Identify a peer who is consistently recognized as being very thorough. Ask the person to tell you what processes/procedures he uses to ensure work is complete and correct. Adapt techniques that make sense for your own job.

• When accepting an assignment or task, ask your manager for the business purpose or objective behind the project. Knowing the broader context enables you to determine and track your work against appropriate measures of success.

• Volunteer to work on projects from the outset or when they are still in the planning stages, instead of waiting to be assigned a task after the planning has already taken place. Early involvement enables you to get a better understanding of the whole project and will help build your commitment to seeing the project through from beginning to end.

• Ask your manager for regular feedback on completed projects and assignments, especially regarding the accuracy and completeness of your work. Draw out specific suggestions your manager may have as to what action steps you can take to become more thorough.

• Use existing processes and procedures that over time have proved to be effective in ensuring the accuracy and completeness of work in your group.

• Get to know the sources in the company that provide you with current, thorough, and accurate information, and avoid those whose information may be outdated, incomplete, or incorrect. Try not to base your decisions and choices on information from the unreliable sources.

• Develop a clear and succinct format for documenting your work so that anyone opening up one of your project or assignment files can easily re-create and make use of the entire process or work plan.

• Develop a process that you can use to make sure you have accomplished all the things needed for a job to be thoroughly done.

• Do advanced planning before jumping in and tackling an assignment or problem. Anticipate what resources and information you will need so that you can be focused on the task at hand. Don't wait to come up with the process for doing the work while you're in the middle of actually doing it.

• Make use of available software tools, and make it your goal to bring such systems on board for your department if you know they will be useful in getting work done in a more systematic manner.

12. *Technical Skills.* You must have or acquire the specific expertise unique to a position or profession.

• Read trade journals, Internet postings, blogs, and specialized technical literature that contains the latest information about areas related to your job.

• Take courses offered by your company, professional associations, and local universities, either in-person or online.

• Seek opportunities to observe, work with, and get feedback from individuals who are highly knowledgeable in specific technical areas.

• Request assignments and tasks that will broaden or increase your technical knowledge. Depending on your job and the knowledge you want to acquire, these assignments may involve more difficult tasks, a greater variety of tasks, new categories of tasks, or areas of greater specialization. Whenever possible, arrange to receive mentoring on these assignments.

• Solicit feedback on your performance. It can be either on your overall performance or the way you handled specific activities or situations. You may want to ask for a more formal appraisal from your manager or peers.

• Let others know what you know. Talk about your work and your willingness to teach others. Many people are overly concerned or embarrassed about appearing superior. As a result, they hold on to what they know rather than share it.

• Build an informal Internet group of peers in similar organizations through which you can exchange ideas and discuss issues relevant to technical advances in your field.

• Aim to take on at least one new project each quarter that will challenge you to search out new ideas and information.

• Attend conferences and trade shows within your professional specialty. Offer to present a paper at a conference or technical symposium on a project you've completed or some research you've done.

• Become a program chairperson for your professional organization's convention or volunteer as an officer of that organization.

• Visit other companies and talk with people in similar functions. Ask them what they do to stay current in the field. After each visit, detail what you have learned.

• Put in your annual goals that you will develop expertise in an area where you do not currently have it.

• Periodically make note of the number of people who come to you with technical questions. Be sure you work with them to teach them how to solve the problem, instead of solving it for them.

• Get published in your field. Start with a trade journal article on a topic familiar to you, or coauthor a paper with someone else.

• Build a career plan specifying the moves that will help you acquire the technical knowledge needed to achieve your goals. Then "shop" your plan around to experts in your field to get their insight and advice.

• Identify a technical mentor you can go to for counsel.

• List the emerging technological advances most likely to have an impact on your field, then develop an action plan to "stay ahead of the curve" and learn about those advances.

- Teach a class in your area of expertise. Remember the old adage, "You don't really understand something unless you have taught it to someone else."

Almost all of the advice in this chapter can be useful to your direct reports, especially the people who show high potential to move up in the organization (and be a credit to you). The action items in particular offer many additional ideas for developing your people.

A Look to the Future

The work world is changing rapidly. One of the most important changes stems from the increasing need to lead across time zones and geographical boundaries. Distance leadership represents a complexity few managers are prepared for. Advances in technology have enabled organizations to locate employees closer to customers, in their homes or clustered together in small offices in other countries. This situation significantly increases the challenges of managing individual work performance because of a lack of face-to-face interaction.

When People Work a World Away

Life used to be so simple. I can remember my first job. I'll bet you can remember yours, too. We used to work in these little boxes. We called them cubicles. Communication wasn't much of a problem. If you wanted to talk to someone, you'd just poke your head over the cubicle. As a manager, you'd make sure people showed up to work, didn't take long lunches, and kept their work area neat and clean. You would actually supervise things. You'd check over people's work to make sure they were doing things right. If not, you'd take immediate corrective action and show them how to do things right. You were in charge. I remember going to business school and being taught that managers control, direct, plan, lead, and organize. Employees simply had to do what they were told. If they were unsure, there was always a manager around to ask. In fact, managers would say, "My door is always open."

Needless to say, things have changed. These days, ask managers a simple question and you get the strangest answers. For example:

Me: How many people work for you?

Manager: Oh, somewhere between five and eighty-two.

Me: That's quite a range. You mean you don't know?

Manager: Well, we have a reorganization pretty much every day. Some people work for me functionally and some directly. Some are company-badged while others are contractor-badged. Some work on a project basis. Some work for four or five managers. Some are part-timers. Some work at home. Some, I don't know who the heck they are.

Many of the managers I know have never met the people working for them because they have never set foot in the employees' country before. Managers who have had difficulty doing the things we've discussed in this book now find themselves having to do these things across cyberspace. There's typically no direction or structure provided in organizations on how to manage people under these circumstances.

Today's manager has to be extremely creative. The organization requires an increasing number of managers to have remote teams, but the infrastructure of the organization usually cannot support these arrangements. For example, performance review systems usually have the same old boxes to check off: Does this person have good work habits? Does the worker take initiative? Are employees good citizens? That's a little hard to determine if the person works in India, Singapore, or China.

In the old days, we'd ask employees what they liked most about their job and they'd usually say, "The other people I work with." In many cases, we've taken that away from people. They work in cyberspace, out of their home or in small offices. People who are remote tend to feel isolated, neglected, forgotten, taken for granted, and out of the loop. They feel like they're "lost in space." Unfortunately, they usually blame their manager for those feelings. Conference calls in and of themselves don't do the trick. The other day I saw someone at a high school football game with two cell phones, one in each ear. When I asked what he was doing, he said, "I'm on two conference calls." I said, "Aren't you going to pay attention to the game? Your son is playing." He responded, "Of course. I'm concentrating on the game. I'm just pretending to be on two calls. You know what work is like. It's all about pretending to pay attention." There are a lot of people out there pretending to pay attention. The problem is that the manager doesn't recognize that people want involvement and engagement. They don't want someone to drone on and on over the phone or in an online meeting.

Once a woman said to me, "My boss is such a control freak. He doesn't belong in today's world." I asked her what the problem was. She said, "We have two conference calls per day with our remote team. He asks everyone to report on their projects one person at a time. So, 95 percent of the call doesn't concern me. It's a complete waste of my time. Each of these calls lasts several hours." I was astounded and asked, "How do you get any work done?" She simply said, "Exactly. That's the problem."

In the manager's effort to try to control the activities of people in remote locations, he is limiting their activities and causing the team to be unsuccessful. That manager and others need to understand that with a remote team, they have to give up control in order to produce success. Managers need the employees to be their eyes and ears. Managers have to realize that they exist only to help the employees to succeed. It's about the remote employees—it's not about the manager. It's as if many managers need to keep repeating the mantra, "In the old days, I used to control things. Now, I'm a helper," until they understand its significance and they practice it.

Remote employees are most like consultants or contractors. You've got to clearly give them your expectations up-front and then let them do their jobs. You trust them, but you also need to set milestones to check their progress. Many of the remote employees I know love the freedom of working remotely. They say, "For the first time in my life, I don't have to ask permission to go to the bathroom or go to lunch. No manager is looking over my shoulder. I feel like an adult. I could never go back to being a colocated employee." For me, as a consultant, I know I get more done in an hour working in my office in my home than I used to get done in a day working in a big office building. I'm away from the interruptions and worthless meetings; I'm not wasting time explaining and defending things to a boss.

The challenge, however, is to still establish and maintain relationships with people who don't work in the same location that you do. The best thing managers can do is brainstorm with their people on how they can be made to feel like a team even though people are in different locations. They'll bring up ideas such as scanning photos of people, or resumes, or job descriptions, and distributing them. Maybe they'll suggest having each person talk a little about themselves at the start of a conference call. They might suggest a team blog, chat room, or website. The sky is the limit. If I were you, I'd support anything that made my team members feel like a team.

Hiring specifications are different for remote employees. If you have someone who likes being told what to do and doesn't want to take initiative, that employee is better off working in an office colocated with more senior people. However, when someone is working remotely and on their own, you've got to have someone who is mature, savvy, assertive, and willing to take initiative. There's not going to be anyone around to tell that person what to do. Unfortunately, if you haven't had to do it already, you may well have to tell someone who you approved to work in a remote situation, "I'm sorry this isn't working out." They may say back to you, "This isn't fair. I've always been a top-rated employee when I was colocated at the main office." You'll have to say, "I know, but this is different. I'm sorry it isn't working out." An average communicator may be okay as a colocated employee but is in trouble in the remote world, both as a manager and as an employee.

Americans are regarded by many people around the world as egocentric. An American manager said to me recently, "I have to deal with these people in India. They speak with a thick Indian accent. I can't understand what they're saying half the time." I pointed out to him, "They're probably saying, 'I have to deal with this American manager. He speaks with a thick American accent. I can't understand what he's saying half the time.'" His response? "There's no such thing as an American accent." Ah, the ugly American. I had another manager who told me that the reason there's so much confusion in the world is that everyone speaks different languages.

His solution? "We should demand that everyone speak English. It's the universal language. Then things will be so much easier." I told him that someone in China is likely saying, "We should demand that everyone speak Mandarin. It's the universal language. Then things will be so much easier." His response? "I'm not going to learn Mandarin. It's too hard."

If you deal with people in other countries, they really appreciate it if you show some interest in them. Just ask about one of their holidays or customs. Learn one word of their language. If you say "Bienvenu" for "Welcome" to someone in France, or "Arigato" for "Thank you" to someone in Japan, they'll be amazed. If you learn who St. Patrick was when you talk to someone in Ireland, they'll think you're terrific. If you have someone on your team whose son plays cricket and you ask how he did in the tournament last weekend, that person will appreciate it no end. It's more important to be an interested person than an interesting person. Most Americans spend their time trying to be interesting and impress others. You'll impress people much more if you're interested in them.

Your Relationship with Others

Assuming you've got a number of people working for you, try listing your direct reports and then their performance ratings. Use the form shown in Figure 13-1. Rate the relationship you have with the employee on a scale of 1 to 5, with 5 being geographically the closest and 1 being the most remote. Then see if you can find common elements between those employees who have the highest ratings and those with whom you have the closest relationship. Assign employees to categories as well, such as colocated versus remote office, experienced versus junior, and old-timers versus those new to the company.

For example, it's very typical to have your "go to" people as those closest to you geographically. After all, they've earned your trust. You know them. They get the choice work assignments, the high-visibility projects, the more challenging work. Those furthest from you are sort of forgotten. At the end of the year, guess who gets the highest performance review ratings? Your go-to people, of course. How do you think those furthest from you geographically feel about that? You can justify your performance rating decision by saying, "Look what these go-to people have accomplished." But recognize that they're the ones you gave the opportunity to. In effect, *you* caused what happens. Maybe everything comes out perfectly and you find that you've been fair to everyone. Maybe you've spent the right amount of time with the right people. If not, complete the action plan (also part of Figure 13-1) to remedy the situation. You may want to do this analysis periodically in order to look at who you pay attention to and the impact it has on their job performance.

The Transition Generation

The other day I asked my teenage son why he doesn't go out and play kickball in the street. I told him that's what we did when we were kids and it was a lot of fun. He sighed and said, "Dad, look at my computer screen." He was instant messaging with fifteen other kids from around the world. They have their own language, their own jargon. They even use an acronym that's texting shorthand for "Be careful what you say. My dad is in the room." How someone could instant message with fifteen other people at once is beyond me. But kids can do it. My son plays adventure games and other computer games with these kids. They're his "friends."

The younger generation will not have the problems we have in dealing with people in cyberspace. They've been brought up with it. They don't know how to do it any differently. We're the ones with the problem. We're the transition generation. We know about the old days of people clustered in little cubicles in big office buildings. We say things like, "How can you give people a sense of being in a team when they're dispersed around the world?" Kids don't know any other way. They're ready for the brave new world. I know managers who say, "If I need ideas on how to communicate with people virtually, I just watch what my kids do." Funny, but kids are the leading edge. We're way behind. We need to catch up.

Keeping Secrets

Some people say that luck is the key to management success. They're right. The better you are as a manager, the luckier you get. With the things you've learned from this book, you'll be able to build high-performing teams that are the envy of people in your company and in your industry. You'll get extraordinary results from ordinary people. You'll have a track record of

Figure 13-1. Assessing your relationship with direct reports and its impact on their job performance.

My Direct Reports	Performance Rating	Relationship	Category
_____	_____	_____	_____
_____	_____	_____	_____
_____	_____	_____	_____
_____	_____	_____	_____
_____	_____	_____	_____
_____	_____	_____	_____
_____	_____	_____	_____
_____	_____	_____	_____

Action Plan

What I realized from this analysis and what I plan to do about it:

_____

_____

_____

_____

_____

_____

significant accomplishments. You'll have an eye trained on the future and the evolving workforce. No one will know how you're able to pull it off time and time again. You'll have a marvelous career and be an icon. They'll probably erect a statue of you in your company cafeteria. You don't have to tell them that all you did was follow the advice in this book. Keep that a secret. Take the credit for yourself. I don't mind at all.

Action Items for Developing Your Ability to Develop Others

Developing People—Challenging, encouraging, and supporting staff members to acquire and apply new and existing knowledge, skills, and abilities to a higher degree of proficiency.

• Encourage employees to share their career goals with you. Once you know their goals, you can help them focus their efforts and plan developmental assignments.

• Provide as much information as you can about positions within the company that may be consistent with each employee's goals. Communicate skill requirements, additional education needs, or experiences that would help to qualify the person for the new position. If you are unfamiliar with the requirements for a particular job, suggest that the employee talk to other people who either currently hold the job or are familiar with its requirements. Be sure to first contact the people to whom you refer an employee to make sure they'll be cooperative.

• Discuss with employees what they know about positions to which they aspire and how their current skills and experience fit with the job requirements. Don't neglect to focus on enrichment, broadening, and mastery of their current job as well.

• If you agree that an employee has the potential to meet his goal, create a development plan together to help him reach the goal.

- If you see an employee's goal as unrealistic given current skill levels, point out where you see discrepancies and suggest other, more realistic alternatives. Make specific suggestions if you can. If not, refer the person to others in the organization who can help.

- When reviewing the career plans of your employees, be sure to consider the following features of a successful plan:

  - *Specificity.* Goals and activities should be stated concretely so that both of you know when objectives have been attained. For example, "Improve your technical skills" is not a specific goal "Earn a Microsoft certification" in a technical skill is a specific goal.

  - *Limited Focus.* Include only a reasonable number of major development areas in the plan.

  - *Commitment.* Employees are more likely to be committed to goals they choose and plans they develop. On the other hand, the goals and plans must fit in with your objectives and those of your team. In addition, you must be committed to providing the opportunities and resources needed by the employee to fulfill the plan. Otherwise development plans become nothing more than bureaucratic busywork.

  - *Small, Reasonable Steps.* Because people grow in small steps, expecting too much too soon can discourage the progress. Divide development activities into small steps that lead to an ultimate goal.

  - *On-the-Job Opportunities.* The most powerful development occurs on the job. It's important that managers and employees use day-to-day job responsibilities as opportunities for development.

  - *Support and Feedback.* Provide support in the form of time, money, reinforcement, and coaching. Tailor your support to the person's learning style.

  - *Specified Time Frames for Accomplishment.* Employees must have an established target date for each task. Schedule dates for completion and use checkpoints to review progress.

• *Adequate Variety.* Employees will be more enthusiastic about plans that include a variety of activities. Ideally, there should be a mix of on-the-job tasks, formal coursework, developmental assignments, and work with professional associations.

• Have an employee accompany you to meetings and then send her as your representative. Be sure that you provide appropriate coaching before the meeting and that your employee understands her degree of authority.

• Examine current and past assignments you've given out. Ask yourself who was assigned to the project, why they were assigned, and how challenging the project was for them.

• Ask if a person performs the same tasks repeatedly or often takes on new responsibilities. Ask if you've given the person opportunities to try new things and develop or enhance his skills. Consider whether you feel the individual has the potential to handle more challenging work. If so, ask what skills, resources, or experiences would help tap his potential.

• Give employees temporary assignments in other groups to enable them to see the business from another perspective. Have them participate in cross-functional task forces, professional conferences, and trade shows. Send them to other companies to benchmark and research "best practices."

• Work with your employees to generate a written operating or communication plan that details how the team is organized, who is responsible for doing what, how the various communication tools will be used, whom to contact on what type of issue, what the expectations are for behavior, etc. Such a written document is particularly valuable for new employees.

Appendix:
Job Satisfaction Survey Details

Nonexempt Job Satisfaction Survey Results
(N = 208)

	Rank order of importance to me in my job (1–20, with 1 the highest)	Satisfaction rating (1–5, with 5 the highest)
Sense of accomplishment	4.27	3.87
Recognition for good work	7.79	3.19
Doing challenging work	6.10	3.17
Pay	5.65	3.02
Sense of competence	9.37	4.26
Status	16.88	3.15
Making use of my abilities	7.51	3.42
Fringe benefits	12.33	3.70
Feeling of personal worth	9.96	3.92
Feeling of belonging	14.96	3.60
Making decisions	13.06	3.01
Promotion and advancement	9.12	2.67
Feeling of achievement	8.38	3.65
Appreciation from others	12.76	3.50
Having responsibility	9.98	3.67
Job security	8.94	2.82
Sense of confidence	9.88	4.09
Friendships on the job	16.46	3.56
Doing meaningful work	11.67	3.83
Working conditions	14.91	3.61
Overall satisfaction with the job		3.60

	Rank order of importance to me in my boss (1–10, with 1 the highest)	Satisfaction rating (1–5, with 5 the highest)
Positive expectations	4.40	3.31
Goal-setting	5.61	3.49
Positive feedback	2.41	3.50
Availability	6.79	2.83
Trust	2.97	3.10
Constructive criticism	9.50	3.24
Providing information	6.11	3.09
Input into decisions	6.26	3.09
Development activities	7.07	3.04
Two-way communication	3.49	3.18
Overall satisfaction with my boss		3.35

Analysis of Nonexempt Results

"Importance to Me in My Job" Ranked by Order of Importance
1. "Sense of accomplishment"—Critical, well met
2. "Pay"—Critical, somewhat met
3. "Doing challenging work"—Critical, somewhat met
4. "Making use of my abilities"—Critical, somewhat met
5. "Recognition for good work"—Critical, somewhat met
6. "Feeling of achievement"—Very important, well met
7. "Job security"—Very important, unmet
8. "Promotion and advancement"—Very important, unmet
9. "Sense of competence"—Very important, extremely well met
10. "Sense of confidence"—Very important, extremely well met
11. "Feeling of person worth"—Somewhat important, well met
12. "Having responsibility"—Somewhat important, well met
13. "Doing meaningful work"—Somewhat important, well met
14. "Fringe benefits"—Somewhat important, well met
15. "Appreciation from others"—Somewhat important, well met
16. "Making decisions"—Least important, somewhat met
17. "Working conditions"—Least important, well met
18. "Feeling of belonging"—Least important, well met
19. "Friendships on the job"—Least important, well met
20. "Status"—Least important, somewhat met

"Importance to Me in My Boss" Ranked by Order of Importance
1. "Positive feedback"—Critical, well met
2. "Trust"—Critical, somewhat met
3. "Two-way communication"—Critical, somewhat met

4. "Positive expectations"—Very important, somewhat met
5. "Goal-setting"—Very important, somewhat met
6. "Information"—Somewhat important, somewhat met
7. "Input into decisions"—Somewhat important, somewhat met
8. "Availability"—Least important, unmet need
9. "Development activities"—Least important, somewhat met
10. "Constructive criticism"—Least important, somewhat met

Overall Satisfaction Scores

*"Satisfaction with the Job itself"—Well met
*"Satisfaction with my boss"—Somewhat met

Exempt Professional Job Satisfaction Survey Results
(N = 307)

	Rank order of importance to me in my job (1–20, with 1 the highest)	Satisfaction rating (1–5, with 5 the highest)
Sense of accomplishment	3.63	3.79
Recognition for good work	6.90	3.35
Doing challenging work	5.67	3.71
Pay	10.25	3.31
Sense of competence	8.82	3.96
Status	15.50	3.10
Making use of my abilities	7.34	3.31
Fringe benefits	15.99	3.18
Feeling of personal worth	7.35	3.75
Feeling of belonging	14.66	3.64
Making decisions	12.85	3.33
Promotion and advancement	10.57	2.98
Feeling of achievement	6.32	3.64
Appreciation from others	11.68	3.44
Having responsibility	9.37	3.44
Job security	12.84	3.31
Sense of confidence	10.05	4.05
Friendships on the job	15.45	3.80
Doing meaningful work	7.44	3.58
Working conditions	16.00	3.57
Overall satisfaction with the job		3.72

	Rank order of importance to me in my boss (1–10, with 1 the highest)	Satisfaction rating (1–5, with 5 the highest)
Positive expectations	4.50	3.26
Goal-setting	5.36	2.83
Positive feedback	3.25	3.21
Availability	7.66	3.56
Trust	3.42	3.79
Constructive criticism	7.84	3.04
Providing information	5.17	3.36
Input into decisions	6.68	3.14
Development activities	6.80	2.71
Two-way communication	4.32	3.34
Overall satisfaction with my boss		3.49

Analysis of Exempt Professional Results

"Importance to Me in My Job" Ranked by Order of Importance

1. "Sense of accomplishment"—Critical, well met
2. "Doing challenging work"—Critical, well met
3. "Feeling of achievement"—Critical, well met
4. "Recognition"—Critical, somewhat met
5. "Making use of my abilities"—Critical, somewhat met
6. "Doing meaningful work"—Very important, well met
7. "Feeling of personal worth"—Very important, well met
8. "Sense of competence"—Very important, well met
9. "Having responsibility"—Very important, somewhat met
10. "Sense of confidence"—Very important, extremely well met
11. "Pay"—Somewhat important, somewhat met
12. "Promotion and advancement"—Somewhat important, unmet
13. "Appreciation from others"—Somewhat important, somewhat met
14. "Job security"—Somewhat important, somewhat met
15. "Making decisions"—Somewhat important, somewhat met
16. "Feeling of belonging"—Least important, well met
17. "Friendships on the job"—Least important, well met
18. "Status"—Least important, somewhat met
19. "Fringe benefits"—Least important, somewhat met
20. "Working conditions"—Least important, well met

"Importance to Me in My Boss" Ranked by Order of Importance
1. "Positive feedback"—Critical, somewhat met
2. "Trust"—Critical, well met

3. "Two-way communication"—Critical, somewhat met
4. 'Positive expectations"—Very important, somewhat met
5. "Information"—Very important, somewhat met
6. "Goal-setting"—Somewhat important, unmet
7. "Input into decisions"—Somewhat important, somewhat met
8. "Development actions"—Least important, unmet
9. "Availability"—Least important, well met
10. "Constructive criticism"—Least important, somewhat met

Overall Satisfaction Scores

*"Satisfaction with the job itself"—Well met
*"Satisfaction with my boss"—Somewhat met

Manager Job Satisfaction Survey Results
(N = 298)

	Rank order of importance to me in my job (1–20, with 1 the highest)	Satisfaction rating (1–5, with 5 the highest)
Sense of accomplishment	4.63	3.82
Recognition for good work	7.53	3.09
Doing challenging work	6.49	3.65
Pay	8.58	3.43
Sense of competence	9.60	3.62
Status	14.21	3.13
Making use of my abilities	8.04	3.40
Fringe benefits	12.62	3.46
Feeling of personal worth	8.31	3.68
Feeling of belonging	12.64	3.53
Making decisions	11.87	3.48
Promotion and advancement	9.13	3.25
Feeling of achievement	8.13	3.42
Appreciation from others	12.35	3.46
Having responsibility	11.05	3.91
Job security	11.95	3.64
Sense of confidence	10.83	3.68
Friendships on the job	14.24	3.57
Doing meaningful work	10.22	3.52
Working conditions	14.21	3.61
Overall satisfaction with the job		3.59

	Rank order of importance to me in my boss (1–10, with 1 the highest)	Satisfaction rating (1–5, with 5 the highest)
Positive expectations	5.09	3.38
Goal-setting	6.18	2.98
Positive feedback	4.81	3.86
Availability	6.61	3.37
Trust	9.67	3.70
Constructive criticism	3.24	3.06
Providing information	5.21	3.40
Input into decisions	5.47	3.32
Development activities	7.72	3.01
Two-way communication	3.89	3.45
Overall satisfaction with my boss		3.38

Analysis of Manager Results

"Importance to Me in My Job" Ranked by Order of Importance
1. "Sense of accomplishment"—Critical, well met
2. "Doing challenging work"—Critical, well met
3. "Recognition"—Critical, somewhat met
4. "Making use of my abilities"—Critical, somewhat met
5. "Feeling of achievement"—Critical, somewhat met
6. "Feeling of personal worth"—Very important, well met
7. "Pay"—Very important, somewhat met
8. "Promotion and advancement"—Very important, somewhat
9. "Sense of competence"—Very important, well met
10. "Doing meaningful work"—Very important, well met
11. "Sense of confidence"—Somewhat important, well met
12. "Having responsibility"—Somewhat important, well met
13. "Making decisions"—Somewhat important, somewhat met
14. "Job security"—Somewhat important, well met
15. "Appreciation from others"—Somewhat important, somewhat met
16. "Fringe benefits"—Least important, somewhat met
17. "Feeling of belonging"—Least important, well met
18. "Status"—Least important, somewhat met
19. "Working conditions"—Least important, well met
20. "Friendships on the job"—Least important, well met

"Importance to Me in My Boss" Ranked by Order of Importance
1. "Trust"—Critical, well met
2. "Two-way communication"—Critical, somewhat met
3. "Positive feedback"—Critical, unmet

4. "Positive expectations"—Very important, somewhat met
5. "Information"—Very important, somewhat met
6. "Input into decisions"—Somewhat important, somewhat met
7. "Goal-setting"—Somewhat important, unmet
8. "Availability"—Least important, somewhat met
9. "Constructive criticism"—Least important, somewhat met
10. "Development actions"—Least important, unmet

Overall Satisfaction Scores

*"Satisfaction with the job itself"—Well met
*"Satisfaction with my boss"—Somewhat met

Bibliography

Adams, J. S. "Inequity in Social Exchanges." *Advances in Experimental Social Psychology*. Edited by L. Berlcowitz. New York: Academic Press, 1965.

Argyris, Chris. *Personality and Organization*. New York: Harper, 1957.

Bennis, Warren. *Organizational Development: Its Nature, Origin, and Prospects*. Reading, MA: Addison-Wesley, 1967.

Bossidy, Larry. *Execution: The Discipline of Getting Things Done*. New York: Crown Publishing, 2002.

Buckingham, Marcus, and Clifton, Donald. *Now, Discover Your Strengths*. New York: Simon & Schuster, 2001.

Buckingham, Marcus, and Coffman, Curt. *First, Break All the Rules: What the World's Greatest Managers Do Differently*. New York: Simon & Schuster, 2001.

Covey, Stephen M. R. *The Speed of Trust: The One Thing That Changes Everything*. New York: Free Press, 2006.

Herzberg, Frederick. "One More Time: How Do You Motivate Employees?" *Harvard Business Review*, January–February 1968.

———. *Work and the Nature of Man*. New York: World Publishing Co., 1966.

Herzberg, Frederick, Bernard Mausner, and Barbara Snyderman. *The Motivation to Work*. New York: John Wiley & Sons, 1959.

Huseman, Richard, and John Hatfield. *Managing the Equity Factor*. Boston: Houghton-Mifflin, 1989.

Landsberger, Henry A. *Hawthorne Revisited*. Ithaca, NY: State School of Industrial and Labor Relations, Cornell University, 1958.

Lencioni, Patrick. *The Five Dysfunctions of a Team*. San Francisco: Jossey-Bass, 2002.

Likert, Rensis. *The Human Organization*. New York: McGraw-Hill, 1967.

Maddi, Salvatore R., and Suzanne C. Kobasa. *The Hardy Executive: Health Under Stress*. Homewood, IL: Dow Jones-Irwin, 1984.

Maslow, Abraham. *Motivation and Personality*. New York: Harper & Row, 1954.

Maxwell, John. *Leadership 101: What Every Leader Needs to Know*. Nashville, TN: Thomas Nelson, 2002.

McClelland, David. *The Achieving Society*. New York: Van Norstrand Reinhold, 1961.

———. "Money as a Motivator: Some Research Insights." *The McKinsey Quarterly*, Fall 1967.

McGregor, Douglas. "The Human Side of Enterprise." *Leadership and Motivation*. Cambridge, MA: The MIT Press, 1966.

———. *The Professional Manager*. New York: McGraw-Hill, 1967.

Mehrabian, Albert. *Silent Messages: Implicit Communication of Emotions and Attitudes*. Belmont, CA: Wadsworth Publishing, 1971.

Merton, Robert. *Social Theory and Social Structure*. New York: Free Press, 1968.

Neff, Thomas, and James Citrin. *You're in Charge: Now What?* New York: Crown Publishing, 2005.

Oncken, William. *Managing Management Time: Who's Got the Monkey*. Upper Saddle River, NJ: Prentice Hall, 1984.

Pfungst, Oskar. *Clever Hans (The Horse of Mr. Von Osten): A Contribution to Experimental Animal and Human Psychology*. Translated by C. L. Rahn. New York: Henry Holt, 1911.

Rosenthal, Robert, and Lenore Jacobson. *Pygmalion in the Classroom*. New York: Rinehart and Winston, 1968.

Skinner, B. F. *Beyond Freedom and Dignity*. New York: Alfred Knopf, 1971.

Vroom, Victor. *Work and Motivation*. New York: Wiley, 1964.

Wagner, Rodd, and James K. Harter. *12: The Elements of Great Managing*. Princeton, NJ: Gallup Press, 2006.

Watkins, Michael. *The First 90 Days: Critical Success Strategies for New Leaders at All Levels*. Boston: Harvard Business School Publishing, 2002.

Index

About the Author

As a training consultant, Len Sandler has developed and delivered more than 2,500 management and professional skills training programs over the past eighteen years. He has worked with such organizations as IBM, General Motors, NASA, Citigroup, General Electric, Honeywell, Motorola, Johnson & Johnson, Pella, SunTrust, Lehman Brothers, AT&T, Disney, EMC, Blue Cross/Blue Shield, Hertz, Sun Microsystems, and Siemens, among others. He has conducted programs throughout the United States and other countries such as in England, Ireland, Germany, Canada, Singapore, Japan, Mexico, and Brazil. Previously, he spent sixteen years in human resources positions, most recently as the corporate HR director at Computervision (now part of Parametric Technology), when the company had 6,000 employees. Formerly an adjunct professor of management at Boston University for fifteen years, he holds a BS in psychology from Boston University, an MBA from Northeastern University, and a PhD in organizational behavior from City University. He is the author of a number of magazine articles, including the award-winning "Successful and Supportive Subordinate." A listing of Sandler's training programs can be found on his website at www.sandlerassoc.com. He can be reached by e-mail at len@sandlerassoc.com.